Curiosities Series

South Carolina
CURIOSITIES

Quirky characters,
roadside oddities &
other offbeat stuff

D1400053

Lee Davis Perry and J. Michael McLaughlin

Guilford, Connecticut

The prices and rates in this guidebook were
confirmed at press time. We recommend,
however, that you call establishments before
traveling to obtain current information.

To buy books in quantity for corporate use
or incentives, call **(800) 962–0973**
or e-mail **premiums@GlobePequot.com.**

All photos by the author unless otherwise noted.
Maps by Gage Cartographics © 2011 by Morris Book Publishing, LLC
Text design: Bret Kerr
Layout artist: Casey Shain
Project editor: Meredith Dias

ISBN 978-0-7627-5996-5

Printed in the United States of America

10 9 8 7 6 5 4 3 2 1

contents

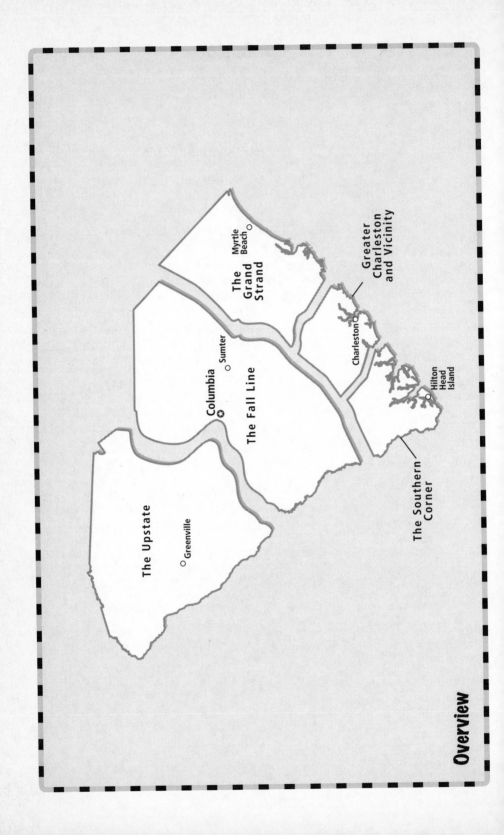

The Upstate

○ Greenville

Columbia ✪

Sumter ○

The Fall Line

The Grand
Strand

Myrtle
Beach ○

Greater
Charleston
and Vicinity

Charleston ○

Hilton
Head
Island ○

The Southern
Corner

Overview

acknowledgments

When we first started writing this book, we were often asked: Where do you find your topics? Our response was *every-where*. But our best ideas came from close to home. What could be better than native South Carolinian family and friends to point us toward some of our state's, shall we say, more unusual attributes?

In this vein Lee would like to thank her family: Joe Perry, Bob Perry, Melissa Sinopoli, Rachel Davis, and Hugh Davis, who provided numerous quirky suggestions and support. Never at a loss for helpful information, old friends Tina and Larry Mayland, Allen Robinson, and new friend Warner Montgomery also sparked ideas for material. Many thanks go out to my cousin, Evelyn Farr, for her invaluable assistance in obtaining photography across the Upstate. Rick Bolt was especially helpful in providing his images from the Lowcountry and beyond. I would also like to commend my coauthor Mike McLaughlin for sticking with this project for the duration in the face of serious health issues. His love for the written word is an inspiration, and his undaunted spirit a source of much admiration. The humor from my husband, Rhett, and interruptions from our dog, Brummy, kept me from some serious computer overload. Many afternoon walks and drives with them forced me to come up for air on a regular basis; I simply couldn't have done it without their loyalty and devotion.

Mike would like to formally thank his coauthor and longtime friend, Lee Perry, for her steadfast support and cooperation during the writing of this book. During much of the creative process I was quite ill and incapacitated. She shouldered her share of the work and sometimes much more (including total responsibility for all photography), which kept the project on target and moving forward. Several times her husband Rhett Perry's unique and humorous perspective on all things Southern saved the day. His warmth and wit lightened our load and brightened the text considerably. Thus, my heartfelt thanks are extended to both Perrys.

We both thank the many museums, visitor centers, and businesses who shared their knowledge and insight into the more unusual attractions, collections, eateries, shops, and festivals around our fascinating state—and they even managed to answer our questions with a straight face.

And lastly, we thank our editor, Meredith Rufino, for her guidance in helping this book come to fruition, and Globe Pequot Press for the opportunity to learn so much more about our beloved South Carolina.

v

introduction

⭐ ⭐

*L*et's start with some basic facts. South Carolina covers an area of 31,113 square miles and is home to about four million people, give or take a few. There are forty-six separate counties, and each one believes it is significantly different from the others. We've been around a long time. For instance, on May 23, 1788, we were the eighth state to ratify the Constitution, which is to say that we had strong opinions at the time, and we didn't shy away from expressing them, and that's probably still true.

There's not much chance of any thorough examination of South Carolina being a bore . . . or a profile of a milquetoast state. This is a place where individualism flourishes and eccentricities rule. For practical purposes we organize the state into five loosely defined categories. First there's Greater Charleston and Vicinity, which is in a category all its own. You'll begin to understand why as you read the chapter. The rest of the state is divided into separate regions based on geography and characteristics like terrain, climate, and population density. We have the Upstate dominated by the Blue Ridge Mountains; the Fall Line (or Midlands), which includes the capital city of Columbia; the Grand Strand, which addresses the Myrtle Beach area and more; and the Southern Corner, which encapsulates the unique world of the vast Lowcountry. On this framework we have attached the following portraits of eccentric people, places, happenings, and history that define South Carolina in a new and refreshing light.

Needless to say, our list of curiosities is incomplete by definition. Oddities are only odd in the eyes of their beholder, but some measures of curiosity are universal, and we think we've aimed close to the target. We hope you like it.

1

Greater Charleston and Vicinity

The problem with *overviews—especially overviews of Charleston—is that they are so unfair. So much gets missed between the lines, and the truth is so bizarre it challenges credibility. In other words you're lost before you get started. But then that's Charleston for you.*

Charleston is an eighteenth-century city that knew great wealth and glory before the fever of independence swept through the colonies. In fact, it was one of the brightest jewels in Mother England's crown. Charleston's crop of patriots, heroes, and statesmen ranks right up there with the best, and yet a hundred years later its substance and swagger gave it the arrogance to secede from the Union, intending to go its own way. And though time, economics, nature's wrath, war, and occupation have taught the city humility, its pride is still palpable and amazingly contagious. That's why four million people come here every year to enjoy its special romantic ether. Charleston has elegant architecture—lots of it— and unbelievable streets, living postcards of yesterday. But the real story is the Charlestonian appetite for beauty in everything. It's a way of life. So naturally, the Charleston experience is also about winsome barrier islands, subtropical breezes through sea oats, and golden marshes. There are swamps, bogs, and tall pine forests that all have something special to say.

No wonder this is a city where eccentricities are encouraged, just as spices are integral to a good recipe. Sorting them out is the hard part, but here are a few that give you a taste of Greater Charleston and Vicinity. We hope you brought a healthy appetite.

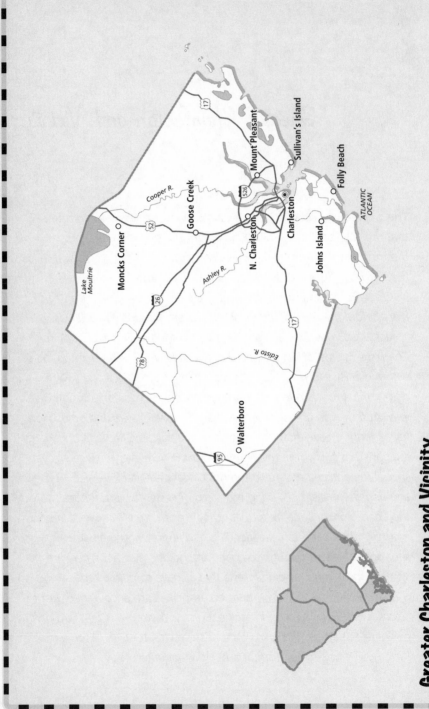

Greater Charleston and Vicinity

Not a palm, but a palmetto tree—an iconic
symbol of a proud and historic state
PHOTO BY RICK BOLT

Terror in Disguise
Charles Towne

For a brief but colorful time in the early eighteenth century, the South
Carolina coast was terrorized by several bands of nefarious pirates.
Names like Edward Teach, "Blackbeard," Stede Bonnet, "the Gentle-
man Pirate," and Bartholomew Roberts, "Black Bart," claim their share
of the fame and later swashbuckling portrayal on celluloid. But nobody
ever talks about the women. Yes, South Carolina had a woman pirate
too, and she was a jim-dandy.

★ ★

Anne Bonney was born in Ireland in the late 1600s, but immigrated with her parents to a South Carolina plantation near Charles Towne when she was still a child. She grew up to be a headstrong young woman with a violent temper and a penchant for having her own way. Against her family's wishes she eloped with James Bonney, a down and out pirate, who also plied the South Carolina waters. They sailed to the Bahamas, where her husband's luck as a pirate did not improve. In fact, when the governor of the Bahamas offered clemency for information leading to the capture of other pirates in the area, James Bonney betrayed his own kind and lost his wife's affection in the process.

Enter Captain Jack Rackam, a dashing, young pirate making a name for himself in the Caribbean. Soon Jack and Anne were inseparable and sailed together on his sloop *Vanity* plying the waters off Cuba and Hispaniola for Spanish gold. Anne Bonney, dressed as a man, could hold her own against the most vicious pirates afloat. Her performance with a sword was as dazzling as it was bloody. She was captured by the British navy and brought back to trial in Jamaica, where she was sentenced to death for her sordid life of crime. Because she was "with child" at the time of her sentencing, her execution was commuted, but from that point on her fate is unclear. Some say she was released and rejoined her father on his plantation in South Carolina and lived out her lifetime there. But no record of her has ever been found to corroborate this rumor. So go the life and times of Anne Bonney, South Carolina's "Lady Pirate."

Arrogance Goes Graphic
Charleston

Several years ago one of the most popular souvenirs sold in the City Market was a poster that was a spoof on a famous cover from the *New Yorker*. The original magazine cover showed the island of Manhattan and a vast wilderness stretching beyond it, all the way to the Pacific Ocean. The Charlestonian version was very similar, showing the historic Peninsula and a vast wasteland extending to the West Coast. This was

4

★ ★

a graphic illustration of one of the oldest Charlestonian clichés, that the Ashley and the Cooper Rivers (flanking the Peninsula) come together to form the Atlantic Ocean. The poster was an instant sellout.

Keeping Up Appearances
Charleston

With all the horse-drawn carriage tours clopping along Charleston's historic streets, tourists are pleased to see that the horses are required to wear diapers. Should a horse's diaper at any time need changing and the street in any way become sullied (they say it happens to even the best of horses), there's a very civilized Southern solution. A special truck patrols the carriage routes during tour hours carrying a large tank of perfumed disinfectant. In case of an accident on the street, carriage drivers are trained to throw out weighted flags to mark the spot and drive on with dignity unruffled. The truck then scurries to the scene for a welcome squirt, a quick wash, and a gracious apology. What can one say? It happens.

Charleston decorum on the hoof

Check Out The Citadel Now
Charleston

The Citadel got a significant amount of unwanted national media exposure in the 1990s during what became known as the Shannon Faulkner debacle. It seems almost quaint today, but single gender institutions, such as The Citadel and Virginia Military Institute (VMI), had mandated a male-only policy that had been in effect since the 1830s. The reasoning, at the time, was that women could not manage the rigors of combat. Of course, alumni that had served in Vietnam knew that women on the North Vietnamese side had been quite effective soldiers.

The Citadel blocked all female applications back then. When the judicial system stepped into the fray, it became a losing proposition for both sides. The first woman admitted could not stand up to the rigors of physical training, which in turn, made matters worse. Fortunately, cooler heads ultimately prevailed; females were welcomed, and have turned out to be not only outstanding cadets, but also fine front line officers.

One year more recently, as a part of pregame festivities at Johnson Hagood Stadium, the game ball was brought in by a HALO unit. HALO stands for High Altitude, Low Opening, where the parachutist free-falls for several thousand feet, and then pops the chute at about a thousand feet. The chute itself is a flying wing, which enables the jumper to sail and glide to offset the vagaries of indigenous wind.

It was a beautiful afternoon, and the public address system directed the crowd's attention to a plane that was flying thousands of feet above the stadium. The crowd could just make out the vague outline of three jumpers as they came out of the plane. After free-falling for quite some time, they released smoke grenades on their boots, each with a different color. There was a spot at midfield that all three strived to hit. The jumpers popped their chutes and came in about thirty seconds apart. As they were gliding down, the crowd took note that the last jumper was trailing an American flag and holding the game ball.

Education at The Citadel today is a far cry
from the military school of the 1800s.

★ ★

The crowd roared when the last jumper hit the mark at midfield perfectly. The jumper handed the game ball to the referee, took off the protective helmet and in so doing let down a full head of bright, red wavy hair and flashed a broad smile. The crowd roared to their feet.

A good time to visit The Citadel is their Friday afternoon dress parade, where you can see the Corps of Cadets in full regalia drilling on the mid-campus parade ground. Visit www.citadel.edu for dates and times.

The Holy City's Holy Cow

Charleston

No teenager graduates from the Charleston school system without learning of the Coburg Cow. The life-size cow accompanied by a giant carton of milk revolves on a prominent sign along US 17 advertising the local Coburg Dairy at the corner of Coburg Road and Savannah Highway. Children see it as a landmark signaling a homecoming after a long trip in the car. Teenagers see it as an opportunity for playful vandalism and over the years have shot it, ridden it, painted it, lassoed it, branded it, and outfitted it in outrageous costumes. Citadel cadets use it as a rite of passage for their own brand of humor, including cap-turing it for interrogation back at the barracks. Savvy advertising types consider the bovine to be solid gold, as no better promotion of the Coburg name could be bought at any price.

So dear is the Coburg Cow to locals that it has been kidnapped by its loving fans on numerous occasions, testing the stamina of the Coburg management to maintain its public presence. Every time it disappears there's a hue and cry from the locals for its return, so that now Coburg is wholeheartedly part of the game. Staff from the dairy maintain a wardrobe of different cow costumes for every holiday. Near Halloween look for a witch's hat, a cape, and a magic broom. At Christmastime the cow's colors change to red and green and a wreath

★ ★

of holly adorns its neck. In the springtime when new life is budding along the roadsides, a pink calf appears beside its loving mother. Although the Coburg Dairy has long since moved to another location, the Coburg Cow stands as a monument to the power of advertising and a city's affection for an icon grown dear to its heart.

The Holy Cow in gobbler garb

Curious Moniker: "The Holy City"

Visitors to Charleston are often confused when locals refer to their home as "The Holy City." Some even take offense thinking it in some way insults the biblical Holy Land of Jerusalem, but no such slight is intended. No one knows for sure when the nickname came into general parlance, but it's widely believed that the term was used by eighteenth-century ship captains, grateful to see solid land after a perilous ocean voyage. Another theory says it has to do with Charleston's tradition of religious tolerance, reflected in the many magnificent church spires that dominate the skyline of the lower Peninsula. Go with one of these stories or make up one of your own.

It's all in the skyline.
PHOTO BY RICK BOLT

The Charleston Eagle, Hardly a Patriotic Icon
Charleston

Every visitor to Charleston sooner or later finds his or her way down to the City Market, which runs from Meeting Street to East Bay. This carnival of colorful sights and sounds and merchandise of all kinds is a Charleston tradition that dates back to the eighteenth century. Originally it was designated as a centralized marketplace for the fish, meat, vegetables, and wares brought in from the nearby wharves and the growing fields outside the colonial city. Before the advent of refrigeration, the butchering was done onsite, and the gutters of Market Street were fouled with the meat trimmings and inedible refuse from each day's knifework. Needless to say, the Market became a smelly and unsanitary eyesore in the heart of the city. But to the rescue came

Nature's sanitation crew at work in the Market
VINTAGE POSTCARD SCANNED BY RICK BOLT

11

Mother Nature's feathered sanitary crew, the less than handsome turkey buzzards, euphemistically described in polite society as "Charleston Eagles."

At the height of the Market's output, the sky over the area darkened with the circling scavengers waiting for another shovel-load of entrails and fish heads. Mercifully, those days are gone, but travelers into the countryside around Charleston occasionally pass the unfortunate scene of a wildlife roadkill. There, feasting away on the malodorous carcass and only momentarily disturbed, is the Charleston Eagle cleaning up the remains of the day and doing his part for a greener, more pleasant American roadside.

Dotting the "I" and Crossing the "T" in Earthquake
Charleston

What are those odd iron symbols that pockmark the facades of many homes and businesses? That's the question thousands of visitors to Charleston's historic peninsula ask when they clip clop through the streets on carriage rides or pass by in air-conditioned buses. The answer is a poignant reminder of a devastating event, the Great Earthquake of 1886, known locally as "The Great Shake." It happened on August 31 of that year, a hot, sultry night, just after most Charlestonians had retired. Experts estimate that the quake was equal to a measurement between 6.8 and 7.7 on the Richter scale. It shook the Holy City to its knees and was felt from the Atlantic seaboard to the Mississippi Valley, from the heart of Alabama and Georgia to as far north as Lake Michigan. Aftershocks continued for days. Ninety percent of the city's buildings were damaged, and 102 were completely destroyed. Almost all of the city's fourteen thousand chimneys toppled over.

Following the earthquake expert federal engineers descended upon the devastated city with recommendations aimed at preventing this tremendous loss of property (as well as lives) from ever happening again. They suggested that "all masonry walls should be securely anchored to the floor, ceiling, and roof timbers with iron anchors"

✶ ✶

Earthquake bolts hold up little more than dignity.

threaded through the walls between the floors. Salesmen offered a
variety of cast iron rods secured with decorative gib plates and screws
with lions' heads, crosses, disks, and stars. Desperate Charlestonians
took this advice to heart and bought the untested earthquake rods
and gib plates by the hundreds and dutifully installed them, trusting
in their protective powers. Considered by most of today's structural
engineers to be virtually worthless, these "earthquake bolts" remain
a ubiquitous presence throughout the city. They are like punctuation
marks reminding proud Charlestonians to pause and reflect upon their
vulnerability in times of duress.

Always Say *Please* and *Thank You*
Charleston

Sometime in the 1980s Charleston was officially named "America's Most Polite City." Ever since, the city has managed to hold onto the title or placed very high in the national rankings. The politeness and gentility that won Charlestonians that title reached *way* back in time. The first fire insurance company in America was started in Charlestown back in 1736, and it was named (be sure to hold your mouth just right) "The Friendly Society for the Mutual Insurance of Houses Against Fire."

Where there was smoke, there was water—if you said please.

The Center of the Universe?

Charleston

The intersection of Meeting and Broad Streets in Charleston is tradition-ally known as "The Four Corners of Law." The old descriptive phrase (mostly mentioned these days by carriage tour drivers and walking tour guides) is meant to imply that you can do literally everything legally required in life right here at this one important intersection. On the southwest corner is federal law, where you can pick up your mail (at the oldest operating post office building in South Carolina). On the south-east corner is God's law, where you can get married (at St. Michael's

The Four Corners of Law holds court at Meeting and Broad.

Episcopal Church, established in 1761, and the place where the visiting George Washington once knelt in prayer). On the northwest corner is county law, where you can pay your taxes (at the Charleston County Courthouse). And on the northeast corner there's city law where, if necessary, you can file for divorce (at Charleston's City Hall, built in 1801). This viewpoint thinly disguises the pride-driven Charlestonian conviction that, indeed, this intersection is the center of the universe.

Fore!
Charleston

America's love affair with the game of golf is no secret—in South Carolina, alone, it's a $1.5 billion industry with some of the country's most famous courses located here. The quality of these courses has attracted several major PGA tournaments watched by millions of fans on television, featuring the biggest and brightest names in the sport.

Somehow the humble origins of the game have escaped common knowledge. Even lesser known is the fact that the first organized golf club in America was formed in 1786, and its members played on a public green (park-like space used by the public) in what is now downtown Charleston. Golfers with a taste for history might like to play a round on that old course called Harleston's Green, but alas, it is no more. Its crowded green has long since succumbed to urbanization, and the club itself has morphed into the Country Club of Charleston across the river on James Island. Even if the old Harleston's Green were still around, modern golfers would have difficulty recognizing anything going on there. First of all the players (men only) sported red coats to stand out among the general public. Not a few of them wore elaborate hats, some adorned with plumes. Harleston's Green was, in fact, a public space crowded with Charlestonians at play. Children playing games, nurses tending to babies, and couples taking the air would confuse today's golfers. Even a spontaneous horse race could erupt at any given time.

The equipment was unrecognizable too. The first golfers played with something called a "feathery," which was a leather pouch stuffed with boiled chicken feathers and sewn into a ball. The clubs used at the time were cupped wooden clubs called "spoons" that resembled today's hockey sticks. Metal irons were not widely used as they had a tendency to burst the bindings on the feathery. The course was different as well with no set tees, no fairways, and no putting greens; instead the players aimed their shot toward a distant hole in the ground, sometimes as much as a foot wide. The location of the hole was signaled by the would-be caddie called a "finder," who chased interlopers off the course in the direction of the play.

As curious as the game was in the early days, refinement in rules, equipment, groundskeeping, deportment, and fashion have brought golf to unheard of heights and the run on chicken feathers has considerably subsided.

Who Says You Can't Take It with You?

Charleston

Eighteenth-century Charlestonians were nothing if not creative with their funerary art. At a time when headstones were imported and expensive, and stone cutters were hard to find, some citizens improvised with the headboard of the deathbed as a graveside memorial to the late departed. Because they were wooden and prone to decay, few of these headboard grave markers have survived into modern times. In the southwest corner of St. Michael's churchyard at Meeting and Broad Streets, you can view a replica of a headboard grave marker, which reads:

IN MEMORY OF MARY ANN LUYTEN WIFE OF WILLIAM LUYTEN
DIED SEPTEMBER 9TH 1770 IN THE TWENTY-SEVENTH YEAR OF HER AGE

The original headboard, made of cypress, withstood the elements for more than two centuries in the open, humid air of Charleston, before it was finally replaced.

St. Michael's Bells: How Sweet the Sound
Charleston

Among the most arresting sights and sounds of Charleston are the
bells of St. Michael's Episcopal Church at the corner of Meeting and
Broad Streets downtown. They ring every quarter hour in a melodic
cascade of tones that sound the same today as when they were first

Connecting the Dots

Who would ever have guessed the
retail signage for liquor stores all
over South Carolina owes its design
to a pack of Lucky Strike cigarettes.
But it's true. And that's only part of the story.

When Prohibition was repealed in 1933, the floodgates opened on
liquor sales, and a political brouhaha ensued over taxation, licens-
ing, and advertising. There were two sides who wrangled over the
issue. The Upstate crowd known as "drys" weren't quite sure that
repeal was a good idea, and the opposing "wets" welcomed it with
open arms. The two factions went head-to-head for nearly a decade.
Finally the state created the Alcoholic Beverage Control Board (ABC)
to regulate and ride herd on this newly unleashed bucking bronco. As
for signage, all retail liquor stores were limited to a small sign only a
few inches high to draw customers inside. A successful liquor dealer
named Jesse J. Fabian took exception to this and commissioned a
sign painter, "Doc" Wansley, to create a sign for one of his Charleston shops in compliance with the new regulation. When the painter
had finished he felt the sign needed embellishment to be noticed,
and he took as an inspiration the pack of Lucky Strikes in his own
shirt pocket. The familiar red dot on every pack of Luckies had been

★ ★

installed in 1764. The eight bronze bells made their first of several long journeys to Charleston across the Atlantic from Whitechapel Foundry of London, England, where they were cast earlier that same year.

Prior to the Revolutionary War, the bells were rung in defiance of the Crown, voicing the city's strong protest against the Stamp Act of 1765. Later, the bells were confiscated by the British and sent back

an icon in the market-place for many years. He painted a bright red circle around the sign, and the rest is history.

The famous red dot took hold across the state and spread like kudzu until 1968. At that time the ABC decreed the red dots to be advertising and therefore illegal, but by now the red dot was part of the land-scape, and the state legislature stepped in

A dot marks the spot where legal spirits are sold.

and saved the day. To this day retail liquor stores throughout South Carolina are designated by big red dots, which attract those looking for liquor and repel those who choose to avoid it.

Bells come home again (and again).

to England as a trophy of war. Once brought to England, the bells ricocheted back to Charleston in 1782 via the generosity of a private investor who objected to this unseemly interruption.

Along came the Civil War and once again the bells were considered at risk, and seven of the eight original bells were sent to Columbia for safekeeping. As every Southerner knows, General Sherman chose Columbia as an artillery target, and the capital of South Carolina was burned to the ground in February of 1865. Only one tenor bell was left in Charleston in St. Michael's steeple to warn the city of encroaching danger. In 1865, the year the city fell, the bell rang dutifully until it cracked.

The following year, the vestry sent the charred bells along with the cracked tenor bell back to the Whitechapel Foundry to be recast in the original molds which miraculously still existed. Two years later, the sounds of "Auld Lang Syne" and "Home Again" rang out over the rooftops of Charleston. The bells of St. Michael's had crossed the Atlantic again to be home (seemingly) at long last.

In 1989, however, Hurricane Hugo scored a direct hit on Charleston, and once more the bells were returned to Whitechapel for yet another recasting. This time the work was part of a $3.8 million restoration and repair of St. Michael's undertaken after the storm. And yes, once again, the original molds were used. The bells returned refreshed and renewed on July 4, 1993, and rang out in a day-long concert of traditional hand ringing done in the English style. Isn't it a pity bells that sound so pretty don't get frequent flyer miles or hazardous duty pay?

John C. Calhoun's "Final Resting Place"
Charleston

One would assume the funeral of a famous public servant and statesman of note would conclude with a dignified burial and that would be that. Not so for South Carolina's inimitable John C. Calhoun, who was a congressman, secretary of war, vice president of the United States, and a U.S. senator. He was planted no less than four times (or more?) before his mortal remains stayed buried once and for all.

His death in March 1850 made headlines all over the country, and plans for a suitable resting place commenced. Because he died in Washington, D.C., he was initially interred in the congressional burial ground in the nation's capital as befitting his position. Daniel Webster and Henry Clay even served as pallbearers. But three weeks later, he was exhumed, and his casket was loaded onto the steamer *Nina*

★ ★

The well-traveled body of John C. Calhoun rests here in
St. Philip's churchyard—or does it?

bound for Charleston. This was done purportedly in accordance with
his wishes. En route he made several stops where he encountered
crowds, honors, and tributes.

Once in Charleston Calhoun was reburied in the hallowed graveyard of St. Philip's Episcopal Church, where he lay under a modest
marble marker inscribed with the single word CALHOUN. Even this was a
temporary resting place while a more elaborate monument was being
planned. But then came secession and the Civil War, which didn't
go particularly well for Charlestonians. By 1863 it looked like the city

might fall. So staunch had been Calhoun's stand for the Southern cause, it was feared his body would be desecrated should Charleston succumb to Northern control. So once again he was dug up and moved to an unmarked, secret location in St. Philip's churchyard across the street.

After the war it seemed safe to return Calhoun to his rightful grave, and so in 1871 he was returned to his original gravesite. Afterwards locals quipped that he crossed the street more times dead than when he was alive. By 1883 again plans were afoot for a more elaborate tomb, and the grave was disturbed once more. The simple marble slab that had marked his grave for thirty-four years was moved to a cemetery wall near his earlier secret resting place. When this was done one would think he could rest in peace, but no, there's more to the story.

A hundred years later an organization called STORCH (Society to Return Calhoun Home) maintained that Calhoun had always wanted to be buried in Fort Hill, now part of Clemson University. Their assertion was that his body had been spirited away in the night to the Fort Hill location, raising doubts as to where Calhoun's remains actually rest. An official investigation showed this was not so, but in 1985 the rumor resurfaced, and it was quickly resolved that the body was indeed still at St. Philip's churchyard.

A few blocks away another memorial to Calhoun stands in Marion Square. There, his likeness is exalted no less than eighty feet into the air where few can gaze into his stern bronze countenance save the pigeons, whose offerings of respect could be misinterpreted.

Beware This Bed-And-Breakfast
Charleston

Charleston's many charming bed-and-breakfast inns enjoy a well-deserved reputation of warmth and hospitality. Little do today's visitors know of the grisly story of Six-Mile House, a roadhouse and inn which once stood at the northern edge of the Peninsula. In the early nineteenth century this inn was the first stop for immigrants heading

★ ★

Lavinia's digs in the Old City Jail still look spooky even today.

to inland destinations in the then sparsely populated state. Exhausted from the long ocean voyage and eager for sustenance and a place to rest their heads, visitors must have seen Six-Mile House as a welcoming oasis in this unfamiliar land.

The proprietors were John and Lavinia Fisher, creative entrepreneurs with a bizarre sense of hospitality. They had a penchant for drugging their unsuspecting dinner guests into stupors and strangling them in their beds later that night. Their motive was robbery, but they were especially heinous in their disposition of the evidence. After stripping the victims of all valuables, the Fishers hauled the dead bodies into the cellar and buried them in lime-filled pits.

No one knows exactly when the crime spree began, but it was unchallenged until 1819 when a more experienced traveler suspected foul play. He narrowly escaped their plot and reported them to authorities. The Fishers' career as innkeepers came to an abrupt halt. In the grim aftermath, between seventeen and twenty-six partially decomposed corpses were found in the cellar. The Fishers were brought to the Charleston City Jail and summarily tried, convicted, and sentenced to death. Not surprisingly their resulting executions were cause for public celebration. Those in attendance recalled a remorseful John Fisher pleading for mercy. But Lavinia mocked the crowd asking, "If any you's got a message for the devil, give it to me quick 'cause I'm about to meet 'im!"

Long after the hanging the ghostly visage of Lavinia Fisher was said to appear in her former jail cell. After the Great Earthquake of 1886, which cracked the walls of the old jail, they say Lavinia's ghost escaped and now wanders the eerie graveyard of the nearby Unitarian Church where she haunts her unmarked grave. (See "Dotting the 'I' and Crossing the 'T' in Earthquake," page 12, and "Mow Less, Love Longer," page 43.)

Strange Guardians of the Peoples Building

Charleston

Pedestrians and motorists passing the tallest building on Broad Street near the historic Exchange Building are often puzzled by the pair of curious animals frozen in stone that flank the front doorway. These guardians are (or were in better days) lions with fangs, claws, and ears alert—ready to defend what was originally the lobby of a now-defunct bank. Time and sandstone and South Carolina's climate are not always happy bedfellows, and over the years, some of the sculptural details wasted away. So much a part of the streetscape had they become by the time the building underwent a recent multimillion-dollar remodeling,

Time-worn, but still on duty

talk of removing the lions spawned an outcry from the locals. Change does not sit well with Charlestonians, so the lions were saved. There they stand today, surreal creatures, mere versions of their former selves, seeing no evil, hearing no evil, and speaking no evil to passersby.

Magnolia: Romance in Repose
Charleston

Charleston's Magnolia Cemetery is the quiet, final resting place of many important Charlestonians and other players in the city's long-running colorful saga. It is also an intriguing collection of Southern funerary art in an almost unbearably romantic setting at the northern end of the peninsula, not far off East Bay Street. The site was originally home to the Magnolia Umbria rice plantation, which existed as far back as 1790. By 1849 181 acres of the plantation on the edge of the marsh had been reserved for a peaceful cemetery, offering badly needed relief to the crowded churchyard cemeteries in the city.

Who said all the pyramids were in Giza?

★ ★

The setting is noted for its ancient live oaks draped by weeping Spanish moss and languid pools over which alligators regularly stand guard. Wild geese, exotic herons, and egrets are frequent visitors to the site. And rare botanical flora bloom in tribute to the dead. There are literally hundreds of ornate family plots, many of which bear famous names. For example you will find the monument of Robert Barnwell Rhett, "Father of Secession," U.S. senator, attorney general of South Carolina, and author. There's also the grave of George Alfred Trenholm, a wealthy cotton broker who served as treasurer of the Confederacy and organized many a blockade run for the cause. Trenholm is thought by some to be the man Margaret Mitchell used as the model for her Rhett Butler.

There is a vast Confederate section with five brigadier generals and more than 1,700 graves of the known and unknown. Eighty-four South Carolinians who fell at the Battle of Gettysburg and the crew of the ill-fated CSS *Hunley,* the first submarine used in warfare, are buried here. (See "Charleston's Forensic Mystery," page 64)

If you go, don't tease the alligators—they take their job as guardians very seriously and have no sense of humor. To find Magnolia Cemetery drive north on East Bay Street (Morrison Drive) and turn right at the traffic light onto Meeting Street (US 52). Turn right at the first opportunity on Cunnington Street and Magnolia's gates (open daily from 8 a.m. to 5 p.m.) are at the end of the street.

Meet and Greet the Hat Man
Charleston

While turning the corner of Church and Broad Streets, visitors can glimpse a remnant of the colorful and vibrant business life that once flourished there in its nineteenth-century heyday. Painted on the side of a building is the curious figure of a man comprised entirely of men's hats—every color, style, shape, and size. He is affectionately known as "The Hat Man."

The Hat Man greets visitors to Charleston and gets double-takes in return.

The original Hat Man was painted as an advertisement for C.C. Plenge, a hat, clothing, and cigar store doing business at that location starting in 1840. The artist was A. Beauregard Betancourt, who started working there in 1872 at the tender age of twelve. In about 1892 it is believed he created The Hat Man as a logo for the haberdashery, which was the oldest hat store in South Carolina. By 1910 Betancourt had assumed ownership. He was a man of eclectic pursuits who was reportedly a ventriloquist, linguist, even vice consul to Argentina. He was well known for drawing and posting in his store window cartoons illustrating current events of the day, and did so until his death in 1944. The Hat Man has appeared ever since on the same corner in various incarnations, even though the haberdashery is long gone. Charleston's intense sunlight, heat, and humidity take their toll, and The Hat Man needs refreshing from time to time.

Lore has it that generations of downtown children learned their numbers by counting the hats while passing by. Today, this beloved figure tips his hat, bidding hello to visitors and residents with a wink to the city's jaunty bygone days.

Peanuts and Personality: Get 'em Here!
Charleston

Lowcountry sports fans soon learn the ins and outs of venues like Johnson Hagood Stadium (home of The Citadel Bulldogs) and "The Joe," the city's baseball park named for Mayor Joseph P. Riley Jr. At about the same time, they get to know a local hawker and marketing phenomenon known as "Tony the Peanut Man." He is Anthony Wright, a fifty-something former factory worker who one day found himself facing the challenges of the unemployment line. When a friend suggested that he sell peanuts for a living, he was incredulous at first. How can anybody make a living selling peanuts, he wondered. With little else to lose he gave it a go, and in short order Tony's contagious grin and salty legumes were a staple offering at local festivals, sporting events, and public gatherings. These heavenly morsels accompanied by a sudsy brew are more popular than ever with today's computer-age sports aficionados.

"Bald" (boiled) peanuts are as Southern as grits 'n gravy, and in no time Tony the Peanut Man had a website and mail-order business, signature T-shirts, and a superhero alter ego now immortalized in a comic book. He may not look like much of a success when he's between the noisy aisles of cheering sports fans, but Tony the Peanut Man is an inspiration to young entrepreneurs and a champion of second chances everywhere. Visit www.tonythepeanutman.com for more nutty info.

★ ★

Porgy: The Man behind the Music
Charleston

Millions of music lovers all over the world have thrilled to George and Ira Gershwin's classic American opera, *Porgy and Bess,* since it brightened the darkest days of the Depression in the 1930s. So mainstream now are the music and lyrics to "Summertime" and "I've Got Plenty of Nothin'" that many fans don't realize the opera was based on a book

Porgy: the myth and the man

penned by Charlestonian Dubose Heyward. Even fewer know that the character "Porgy" was based on a real man.

Samuel "Goat" Smalls was born in 1889 on James Island across the river from Charleston, one of twenty children born to Elvira Smalls, in a small clapboard cabin, originally built for slaves. Early in Sammy's childhood, he lost the use of his legs, probably due to spinal meningitis. From that time forward he never walked again. He got around by dragging himself along with his arms and using a crude makeshift cart, hitched to a goat. Because of this his life was confined to the streets and alleyways of the downtown Peninsula, and he became a familiar figure to Charlestonians in the 1920s. Heyward's poignant love story features the tragic romance between Porgy and his drug-addicted Bess.

In a quiet graveyard on James Island, Sammy Smalls was all but forgotten. In 1987, more than sixty years after his death, a self-appointed committee of downtown Charleston businessmen erected a memorial headstone over the man's unmarked grave. It reads: SAMMY "GOAT" SMALLS . . . THE INSPIRATION FOR DUBOSE HEYWARD'S NOVEL *PORGY*, AND LATER THE OPERA, *PORGY AND BESS*, BY HEYWARD AND GERSHWIN.

To visit the site take Folly Road to James Island Presbyterian Church and turn left at the traffic light onto Camp Road. Enter the church parking lot, and the marker is to the left just outside the churchyard gates.

Huge Bridge Bows to Tiny Problem
Charleston

In the summer of 2005, the dedication of the Arthur Ravenel Jr. Bridge over the Cooper River was a major event for Charleston and the entire Lowcountry. Indeed, it was a major economic boom as a construction project. It involved ten years of planning, generated thousands of employment opportunities, and cost $632 million. When finished, it provided our growing port with easier transportation to multiple markets throughout the Southeast. This engineering marvel and technological feat became the longest cable-stayed span in all of North America.

What is now high drama crossing the Cooper River was high anxiety on the old 1929 bridge.

Great as the opening celebration was, a certain lump remained in the throats of older locals who will always recall the two former spans, the (1929) Grace Memorial Bridge and the (1966) Silas Pearman Bridge. Each in its own time was considered a miracle of engineering. Each brought a vast improvement to the Lowcountry lifestyle.

Ground was broken for the new Arthur Ravenel Jr. Bridge in July 2001. From the very beginning construction went well, and the span with its eight lanes and fifteen ramps was completed well ahead of initial projections. It made the key travel connection between Charleston's Crosstown Connector and Johnnie Dodds Boulevard in Mount Pleasant, a distance of three and a half miles. Its main cable span is

★ ★

1,546 feet long. The two diamond-shaped tower piers include viewing platforms stretching twelve feet out over the water at a breathtaking height of 198 feet. All this is suspended by 128 individual cables—each one capable of carrying over a million pounds, or five hundred tons. A twelve-foot-wide bicycle and pedestrian lane has become a huge hit with local athletes and pedestrians alike. A lot of its appeal has to do with the spectacular vista of the city's skyline and harbor.

During most of the year, tourists marvel at how handsome the Ravenel Bridge looks at night. But during the nesting season of the Lowcountry's endangered loggerhead sea turtles, the bridge's lights are subtly turned down. It seems the fragile young hatchlings are guided by moonlight in their life-or-death scramble from beachside nests to the relative safety of the sea. Wildlife experts fear the massive bridge lights may compete with the real moon and confuse them. Sometimes the big guys have to give it up, so the little guys have a chance.

Shopping for the Past
Charleston

Charleston's legendary King Street has been a fascinating avenue of commerce for nearly three hundred years. The goods and products that created much of the Charleston lifestyle have been carried in and out of these storefronts for generations—everything from ship's chandlery, fine furniture, and imported books and spices, to the latest fashions from London. Today, much of yesterday's commercial parade has marched on by and lives only in colorful memory. In its place is a homogenized blend of nationally known retailers with famous names. However, one holdover is Read Brothers at 593 King Street, a survivor from the early-twentieth-century heyday when upper King Street was a retail wonderland with ethnic diversity and a thriving local patronage.

Neither a traditional five and dime nor a department store per se, Read Brothers is an indescribable mixture of all that merchandise and more, combined with nostalgia and atmosphere to boot. It simply must be seen to be believed. Starting with the window displays

Step right in, yesterday for sale.

outside, you can see an array of fabric draped in artistic poses with a smattering of merchandise here and there, but you're still unprepared for the cornucopia of items that await your shopping pleasure inside. Display cases from before the world wars create aisles where the dominant merchandise appears to be fabrics and imported goods from all over the world, none of which seem to be related. You can also find things like artists' canvases, musical instruments, and Caribbean metal art. Handmade items from Mexico may be next to batiks from India, next to colorful awning fabrics, next to the finest satin ribbons and fringe. Just when you get your bearings, you learn there's a room to the side with state-of-the-art electronics and video equipment for the most sophisticated audiophile.

Don't expect to be smothered in over-attentive service; you'll appreciate the time to browse around. Eventually you'll be waited on politely, and everything you buy will be rung up on a vintage cash register that may date to when Read Brothers first occupied the store in 1912. The musical "ka-ching" it makes with every sale is a charming visit to the past and a shopping memory most worthwhile. For more visit www.readbrothers.com or call (843) 723-7276.

Beware of Low-Flying Tourists
Charleston

If the above warning isn't said out loud by Charlestonians every winter when the Southeastern Wildlife Exposition (SEWE) is in town, it certainly is what they are thinking. Suddenly out of nowhere in mid-February thousands upon thousands of wildlife enthusiasts descend upon the city for a three-day extravaganza of art, solely focused on the outdoor sporting life. This swarm of nature lovers isn't just from South Carolina. They're wildlife junkies from all over the South and beyond, even a few foreign countries. People walk around in their full camouflage hunting regalia and more often than not, they bring along their dogs. Labs, spaniels, and retrievers parade up and down the streets with their proud owners in tow and woe be to anyone or anything that gets in their way.

Don't misunderstand, South Carolinians love dogs. In fact, as you wander throughout the state, you will notice that almost everyone has one. Every fine Son of the South has a couple of pictures of his dog in his wallet along with his children. Everyone has a story about how smart his or her dog is. A fine upstanding lawyer in the Lowcountry was heard to observe, "I just hope I turn out half as good as my dog thinks I am."

When SEWE is in Charleston, one of the biggest draws for the public is the dog demonstrations. They are not "pretty" dog shows like the one in New York at Madison Square Garden. These are working

A South Carolina hunting dog's work is never done.

exercises where you can enjoy watching fine retrieving and jumping competitions. The Labs get a running start and launch themselves on a horizontal plane into a tank of water in hot pursuit of a decoy. It is not unusual to see a Lab or a Golden jump twenty feet. The retrieving demonstration is a blind retrieve using only hand signals. There is a lot more to the Wildlife Expedition than just dogs performing. You'll find photography, prints, and paintings along with sculpture, carvings, collectibles, and crafts. Check out their website, www.sewe.com, for a schedule of events, exhibits, tickets, and accommodations.

How Do You Guys Say It?

When in Charleston pronouncing certain Lowcountry names can be treacherous. Just when you think you know how something is said or spelled, you encounter a local eccentricity that defies logic. To wit: Legare Street is pronounced "Le-GREE," Hasell Street reads like *hassle* but is pronounced "HAY-zel." Farther afield Beaufort is pronounced "BEW-furt," and in North Carolina they bristle unless you pronounce it "BOW-furt." If you get confused, ask any local—they're sure to have it all down pat.

Once you find your street, then you learn how to say it.

✳ ✳

Scribblings of Fame

Charleston

Among Charleston's many fascinating museums, perhaps the most surprising is the Karpeles Manuscript Museum at 68 Spring Street (at Coming). Off the main tourist path, this gleaming white temple was originally built as a church. Today it houses a collection of historic documents compiled by philanthropist David Karpeles, a Minnesota-born real estate magnate. It is one of a number of locations throughout the country showcasing Karpeles's formidable accumulation of manuscripts acquired over decades.

History lives here.

Revolving exhibits feature documents from the worlds of history, exploration, cartography, religion, art, music, politics, literature, and even medicine. Seeing the actual handwriting reflecting great moments in history illuminates the event's humanity in a way that is both unexpected and arresting. Don't be surprised to find treasures such as Abraham Lincoln's original draft of the Emancipation Proclamation or the handwritten United States Bill of Rights, and personal correspondence from the likes of Gandhi, Napoleon, Walt Disney, and Mary Queen of Scots.

Karpeles's collection was initially inspired in the late 1970s when his family was visiting an art museum in Pasadena, California, where his son encountered a letter penned by the actual hand of genius Albert Einstein. The boy was struck by the fact that the document was self-edited, tentatively reworded in many places, and generally a mess as far as penmanship goes. In short the boy discovered Einstein may not have been so different from himself. He wanted to know more; he was inspired, he learned. The usefulness of a manuscript museum became evident to Karpeles, and the concept of the Karpeles museum was born.

Today the vast collection circulates through nine locations around the country often organized into themes like nineteenth-century authors, motion picture moguls, and rock stars. Admission to the museum is free and open to the public; adjacent parking is provided. Call (843) 853-4651 or visit www.karpeles.com for more.

Charleston's SOBs
Charleston

Anyone visiting downtown Charleston quickly hears about the difference between what's north of Broad Street and what lies to the south. Above this line of demarcation is a world known as "Above Broad," and it means nothing more than what it says. The area below that line is widely known as "South of Broad," which is frequently abbreviated to "S.O.B." Those who proudly live "S.O.B." are quick to say it has nothing whatsoever to do with the descendants of female dogs;

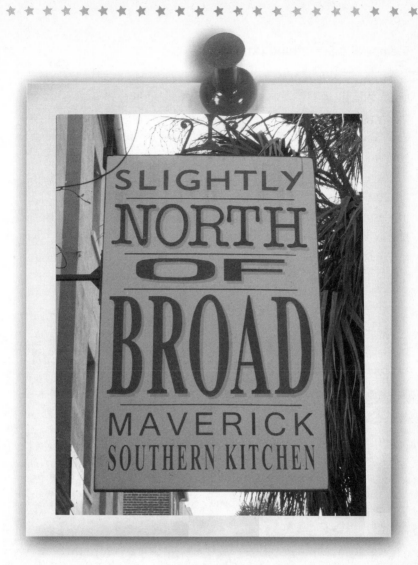

The Slightly North of Broad (S.N.O.B.)
Restaurant is popular with SOBs.

rather, it alludes to a multigenerational lifestyle of privilege, grace, heritage, and affluence that has been a sobriquet for all things Charleston for more than two hundred years. If you doubt this, just ask 'em.

★ ★

Stamps and Something Extra

Charleston

If you stop by the U.S. Post Office at Meeting and Broad Streets to
mail a postcard home or pay a bill, you don't expect a history lesson to
boot. But the Charleston post office offers an unexpected gem that's
well worth seeing.

The Postal History Museum is a special room tucked into one of
the corners that shows visitors some of the interesting postal history associated with this coastal colonial town. Charles Towne's first
postmaster was on the job before 1694, and he was required to
post incoming letters in a public room in his house for thirty days. He

Mail Call: Charles Towne, America

collected his commission only when the letters were picked up by the recipients. Amazingly, this system worked. People in London in 1700 could address a letter to "John Doe, Charles Towne, Carolina," and it would safely arrive. Letters on display prove it. You'll also see letters that survived British occupation, the Revolutionary War, the Civil War blockade, and any number of other calamities. This little museum is a must for philatelists or anyone who ever wondered how eighteenth- and nineteenth-century mail was handled. It is open during regular post office hours and admission is free. It's also a great excuse to see Charleston's elaborately detailed 1896 post office building, the oldest continuously operating post office in the Carolinas.

All That Jazz
Charleston

Everyone seems to know a step or two from the 1920s dance craze that swept the country and set the tone for America in the Jazz Age. It was called, of course, "The Charleston." What relatively few people know, however, is that the dance is culturally attributed to a group of orphaned boys who played band instruments on the steps of Charleston's Jenkins Orphanage in 1892. The orphans played and danced for passersby who tossed coins in appreciation for their efforts. From these modest origins came the careers of several jazz greats and a dance phenomenon that has endured for nearly a century.

Mow Less, Love Longer
Charleston

Charleston's many historic churchyards have spawned nothing short of an industry in cemetery tours, ghost walks, and mysteri- ous tales. The graveyard that always catches visitors off guard is the burial ground beside the Gothic Unitarian Church on Archdale Street. People are struck by what seems to be benign neglect as the grounds appear overgrown in a tangle of briars, vines, weeds, and flowers gone to seed. Nothing could be further from the truth. The

★ ★

Time's garden—overgrown with love

congregation jealously guards this horticultural chaos as a time cap-
sule of nineteenth-century funerary art and botanical tributes to loved
ones long gone. Many of these wild plants and flowers are almost
forgotten varieties not found in any seed catalog or florist's inventory
today. Somehow the tangle amid the gravestones makes a statement
in aggregate about what was and what still is in life itself. To some
it's an acquired taste, but to others it's a rare and refreshing tribute to
those lying undisturbed by noisy mowers and flailing Weedeaters.

Whale of a Tale
Charleston

Charleston has long harbored the dubious distinction of being a closed society. That is, the elite of the city belong to a world and a lifestyle that is inaccessible to outsiders of any stripe. One cannot gain access to this world through any conventional means: not through deed, marriage, fame, and most importantly—wealth. One must be *born* to it.

The greatest metaphor for this indisputable rule hangs from the ceiling of the Charleston Museum on Meeting Street (across from the

A rude intrusion—cut to the bone
COURTESY OF THE CHARLESTON MUSEUM, CHARLESTON, SOUTH CAROLINA

★ ★

Charleston Visitor Reception and Transportation Center). There, just inside the front doors, hang the bleached bones of a giant sperm whale that had the sad misfortune to wander into Charleston Harbor in early January of 1880. Whether the mammal was sick, disoriented, lost, or socially ambitious has never been recorded, but to Charlestonians the interloper was apparently an affront to their genteel sensibilities.

Inspired by righteous indignation the locals set out in a fleet of steamers, tugs, sailing craft, and rowboats. The battle ensued for the better part of the day, but in the end the erstwhile Charlestonians prevailed; they dutifully ensnared, harpooned, and clubbed the poor creature to death. In triumph they hauled the mighty carcass onshore as a trophy of victory. For a dime locals could visit the mammal and marvel at its audacity. Eventually, this enterprise went the way of all flesh and a better resting place was sought for the remains. Then, as now, the Charleston Museum collection consisted of curiosities and wonders from the world at large gathered and displayed for the edification of the community. There among stuffed camels, prehistoric shark teeth, and an Egyptian mummy hang the bones of this errant social climber from 1880.

The moral of the story seems clear. The city fathers are sending a message for all newcomers and would-be aspirants to the rarified airs of Charleston society: "Admission is politely restricted, or in other words, not in my harbor, you don't."

Chew on This One
Charleston/Boston

It would seem logical that the chocolate-wrapped vanilla nougat candy bar known everywhere as the Charleston Chew originated down in Charleston's market area, where colorful vendors sell all manner of goods and tasty delights on a daily basis. But then again logic rarely has anything to do with it. The Charleston Chew was actually invented by the Fox Cross Candy Company in Everett, Massachusetts, near Boston. The year was 1922, and America was intoxicated by the dance that originated in Charleston, South Carolina, named after the city of its birth. (See "All That Jazz," page 43.) The Bostonians named their candy the Charleston Chew to piggyback on the popularity of the dance craze sweeping the nation. Sales figures for the candy grew and soon the comic books of two early superheroes, Wolverine and Spider-Man, were sponsored by Charleston Chew.

By 1957 Fox Candy had been sold to Nathan Sloane, who expanded the product line and its national distribution. In turn the candy caught the eye of Nabisco in 1980, who then sold it in 1993 to Tootsie Roll Industries. This seemed like a happy marriage as Charleston Chew and Tootsie Roll are both a chewy challenge for the jaw.

Charleston has always boasted about being a city of many firsts. But this time they missed the boat entirely, and even money says Boston isn't likely to let Charleston ever forget it.

Flavor and Fun by the Shovel-Load
Folly Beach

The place known as Bowen's Island restaurant is funky. Really, really, funky. And that is what makes you want to go back time and time again. There are quite a few things that it is not. It is not, thank goodness, a four-star restaurant, although the oysters are succulent, tasty, and to die for. The ambience is not the norm for a seafood restaurant, but that is the point. It's not a restaurant, it's a joint. And yet, the ambience makes it what it is.

In the '60s, you couldn't get to Bowen's Island at high tide, because the water covered the road. There was no indoor plumbing, and no chair or table matched. There was a collection of old TV sets stacked on top of each other, where the picture came out of one and the sound came out of another . . . and then there was the jukebox, an old one that played 78s, and the newest record on it was "The Yellow Rose of Texas." And there was the guest book. It read like *Who's Who in America,* with movie stars and national politicians along with everybody else.

★ ★

No coat, no tie, just fun

In the old days, Mrs. Bowen ran the joint with an iron fist. One quickly learned that she made the rules, and you had to obey her protocol. Some coed always wanted to eat shrimp in the Oyster Room, but that was a big no-no. Mrs. Bowen would unceremoniously throw her out. Only oysters could be eaten in the Oyster Room, end of discussion. Tables were covered with old newspapers, and the guy who cooked the oysters shoveled them onto the tables along with some dippin' sauce and saltines. Cold beer and that was it. When you were through shuckin' and eatin', the cook would shovel the empty shells out the window . . . not great for style points but very efficient.

The crowds on the weekends were mostly on the raucous side. They had come to drink beer, eat oysters, and watch a soundless black and white TV while "The Yellow Rose of Texas" played over and over. For fifty years or so patrons had scribbled all over the walls, just to remind others that they had been there.

But good things just don't last forever. Mrs. Bowen died, and her grandson, Robert, took over. He had the good sense not to change anything. But tragedy struck again when the main building burned down, and with it, the guest book, old newspapers, furniture, TV sets, and the jukebox. Life is not fair. Robert has remounted and reloaded. He rebuilt the restaurant on the same site, and fortunately, for all mankind, he has kept it funky.

There are only two other places on the coast of South Carolina where you can get oysters like these: McClellanville is one, and Bluffton is the other. But Bowen's Island is in a class by itself. Take Folly Road (SC 171), look for their sign, and turn right. Call (843) 795-2757 for more.

Hugo's Roadside Legacy
Folly Island

The devastating effects of Hurricane Hugo on September 21, 1989, have left physical, mental, and financial scars all around the Lowcountry. But one of its reminders has made the transition from trauma to something whimsical and fun. The 135 mph winds and on-rushing storm surge deposited a forty-foot-long World War II–era lifeboat of unknown origin on the roadside between James Island and Folly Beach. It still rests there pointing eastward at a rakish pitch on land partly on Folly Road right-of-way and partly in the marsh. Its serendipitous position is such that jurisdiction over the boat is jointly shared by the State Department of Transportation, the South Carolina Department of Health and Environmental Control, and the City of Folly Beach—in other words it's everybody's boat, and it has become nothing short of a community billboard.

Within weeks graffiti started appearing on the hull as an expression of post-storm frustration and relief, and a local tradition was born. Ever since, unknown persons with colorful imaginations have used the boat as a canvas for their folk art, leaving messages, monikers, and memorials for passersby. The artists come in the dark of night so their

★ ★

Folly boat: washed up but not washed out

work is usually anonymous. The messages change almost daily; in fact, it has been said they change with the tides. In Day-Glo spray paint birthdays have been celebrated, love has been professed, marriage has been proposed, the birth of children announced, and the dead have been memorialized. It's especially busy around election time; no candidate's campaign is completely viable without an endorsement on the Folly boat hull. Once it was even entirely painted pink to remind drivers of the battle against breast cancer. The untold layers of paint seem to suggest this roadside curiosity has a legitimate purpose and a public following that will endure. It may not be fine art, but it's an appropriate welcome to quirky Folly Island, known as the Edge of America.

South Carolina's Fractured Syntax, Similes, and Broken Malaprops

Here in South Carolina we speak a foreign language to most folks from off (away from here). You will notice that we almost never pronounce "r" like they do in Cleveland. We say "ah" instead. It is not "never before"; it is "nevah befo-ah." It's not "up the river"; it's up "da rivah." Down in Charleston they have their own way of saying things. For example Huger Street is really "You-gee" and Fort Moultrie is "Fote Moo-tree." We routinely drop "g" as if it never existed. She's my "kissing cousin," becomes she's my "kissin' cuz." In the Lowcountry they aren't "peeling shrimp," they're "peelin' 'em." It's not a matter of being lazy; it's just the way South Carolinians talk.

Elsewhere it's not uncommon to hear colorful comparisons like "he's two french fries short of a Happy Meal," "he's home but the porch light is off," or "I just don't think he's wrapped real tight." Our comparisons tend to be a little sweeter and more gentle. They veritably drip with Southern charm. To wit, if a lady happens to be really attractive, instead of whistling at her like they do in New Yawk, we say, "She'd make a little dog break a big chain."

In the not-too-distant past, a fellow from Beaufort was asked, "How's your day going?" and to no one's surprise, he said, "I've got too many irons in the water." Then came, "Is that the same thing as having too many oars in the fire?" Or "A bush in the hand is worth two birds." Or "you can lead a horse to water but you can't fool all the people all the time." And the classic retort, "It's the zack same thing, buddy boy, the zack same thing."

Got (Goat) Milk?
Goat Island

Whether or not the story of Goat Island is based on fact is anybody's guess. After so many years of retelling, whatever might have been true has grown to heroic proportion. It's another case of time and amplification mixed with wishful thinking.

In the early days of the Great Depression when millions of Americans were disenfranchised from mainstream society, people were hungry for alternative lifestyles. One couple in South Carolina chose to reject the economic woes of the day and retreat to a small barrier island two hundred yards west of the Isle of Palms. At the time this island had no electricity, running water, or anything else for that matter, except for a small herd of goats who were captive there. No boat made a regular call and, although it was easily seen from the Isle of Palms, this little slice of paradise was completely isolated from modern life. Henry and Blanche Holloway lived an *au naturel* lifestyle alone on the island with no company other than a few goats. Somehow they managed to sustain themselves drinking rainwater and eating the natural vegetation growing on the island. They were warmed in the winter by driftwood fires, and in the summer they stayed cool under the shade of palm fronds. They were just far enough away to be mysterious and just close enough that people knew they were there. In fact neighbors on the Isle of Palms, catching an occasional glimpse of the reclusive couple, started calling them the "Goat Man" and the "Goat Woman." Of such stuff legends are made.

Before long the word spread in Charleston and on the Isle of Palms that the Holloways had lost their minds, and people simply left them alone. To social-minded Charlestonians, life without cocktail parties and debutante balls was beyond imagination. Thirty-two years passed (but who's counting?), and time and tide caught up with Henry. His death from pneumonia left Blanche by herself for almost a year. When she followed him to the grave, they were buried together in the cemetery of a Mount Pleasant Lutheran church.

The Holloways' private paradise has slowly gone the way of all barrier islands—into the throes of development. Even the goats are gone. But youngsters playing near the shore of Goat Island today still search for traces of the mysterious Goat Man and his Goat Woman. Imagination is a powerful thing.

Anchors Aweigh for Underwater Archaeology
Goose Creek

It's no surprise to most South Carolinians that the soil under their feet is fertile ground for archaeologists. Everybody seems to acknowledge that the Lowcountry was the first area to be settled by the Europeans in the seventeenth century. What is lesser known, however, is that the waters surrounding this land yield equally fascinating artifacts that illuminate the colonial era's dependency on water transportation. Fewer people still know that an underwater archaeology trail exists on the Cooper River, accessible to scuba divers of moderate skills who agree to exercise prudent safety procedures around these valuable historical sites. The genesis of this underwater museum is a curiosity unto itself. Artifacts like centuries-old anchors and the remnants of early vessels are enormously expensive to conserve and display above ground. On the other hand, the underwater environment preserves the artifacts and allows them to be accessed by divers in situ for many years.

The Cooper River Underwater Heritage Trail, just north of Cypress Gardens and extending up to Mepkin Abbey (see "Spiritual Makeovers Done Here," page 58), includes the Strawberry shipwreck of 1781, the Strawberry Ferry Landing built in 1705, the Pimlico sailing vessel, a nineteenth-century barge, the Mepkin Abbey boat, and a former plantation wharf. So far the trail consists of a number of historic anchors gleaned from ships, utility vessels, and river barges that once plied the Lowcountry waters. The artifacts rest in about twenty feet of water where visibility ranges from two to twenty feet depending on the tide. The trail is marked by guidelines, buoys, and underwater plaques. Interested divers looking for an unusual adventure may call any of the local Charleston area dive shops for an organized charter.

★ ★

Hugo Nevermore

Finally, the weather forecasters have started retiring the names of storms that have become hurricanes of mass destruction. This is a very good idea. There will never be another "Gracie" for instance, never another "Andrew" and please, God—never another "Katrina." There will be other storms, but at least they won't have those particular names. The list of potential names is unlimited, of course, so there will never be a storm that is anonymous. But while we are at it, let's nominate the name of "Hugo" for this never again status. Anyone who was in the Carolina Lowcountry on September 21, 1989, will second the motion and revile the name. Hurricane Hugo was three hundred miles wide with 135 mph winds and a devastating storm surge. It changed the lives of millions of South Carolinians and did millions more in damage. It's not the name that's so offensive; it's the storm's aftermath that is unpleasant to recall. Here's an idea: Let's retire the concept of hurricanes instead. All in favor, say "aye."

Froggy Went A-Courtin'
Johns Island

Out of the mysterious marsh that surrounds South Carolina's barrier islands have crawled more than alligators, snakes, and otters. This swampy birthplace has rendered a monster or two for the movies and late-night TV shows, but the oddest thing to come out of these briny estuaries and salt marsh nurseries are the sculptural frogs of artist Charles "Frog" Smith. From his hermit-like studio on a family island somewhere south of Charleston, Smith has created a genre of art all

★ ★

his own. Smith's life-size frogs fashioned of copper, brass, and stainless steel have been leaping into prestigious galleries all over the South since 1974.

Charles Smith had retired from a career in engineering and science before he started making serious sculpture. "Natural subject matter, coupled with the basic desire to render the life-size image of the human form in metal are the forces that led to the copper frog," is how Charles himself put it. As a result the frogs he's now famous for bear an uncanny "aliveness." They sit contemplatively and lounge on chairs while smoking or sipping a martini. They read books, chase fireflies, and play several musical instruments. They've been installed

Not exactly lifelike—but charmingly human in habit and pose

in manicured gardens, schools, libraries, living rooms, and lobbies, and pose with amusing nonchalance.

So popular have these frogs become in the last few decades that Charles's son, Zan, has grown up with them and has become a "frog-smith" as well. Zan works independently and frequently collaborates with his father on special projects. Over the years they have developed a special process for giving the art a verdigris patina that adds distinction and a certain authenticity as if the sculpture has just emerged from the odorous pluff mud of a South Carolina creek.

These days Charles and Zan Smith's frogs (and other wildlife sculptures) most likely can be found at the Hamlet Fine Art Gallery at 7 Broad Street in downtown Charleston, or at the Carolina Clay Gallery at 565 Freshfields Drive on Johns Island. Visit www.hamletgallery.com or www.carolinaclaygallery.com for more information.

The Angel Oak, Wonder of the Woodland
Johns Island

One of the hardest jobs for tour guides in Charleston is to sell visitors, dazzled by the city's architecture and other attractions, on the idea of driving to Johns Island to see a tree. But it's not just any tree, it's an *old* tree, and one that remembers more than tongues can tell.

The live oak (*Quercus virginiana*) is native to the Lowcountry and especially common on the Sea Islands. They were aggressively harvested by early settlers for shipbuilding, so ancient specimens like the Angel Oak are nearly extinct. Even after hurricanes, wars, wildfires, and (fiercest of all enemies) threats of development, this tree still stands. It is sixty-five feet tall, but its circumference is twenty-five and a half feet, providing an incredible seventeen thousand square feet of shade under its spreading bowers. Its largest arm is eighty-nine feet long and eleven feet around.

Live oaks are difficult to date as they rot from the core as they age, making the counting of rings unreliable. But here's what's amazing: Some estimates are that the Angel Oak is fourteen hundred years

The outstretched arms create virutal "rooms" for worship, contemplation, gatherings of celebrants, and nature lovers.

old or more. It is said to be the oldest living thing east of the Mississippi. It has been attracting awestruck admirers under its leafy arms for eons. Something about that fact gives the scene an almost sacred air. Indeed, Native Americans (of the Kiawah tribe) held ceremonial events there, and freed blacks on Johns Island, Seabrook, and Kiawah used the tree for their church services. It's fun to picture these colorful events and even more fun to picture it as the setting for contemporary dance events including ballet performances during Charleston's

★ ★

Spoleto Festival in the spring. During one performance of the "Rites of Spring" the wood nymphs were frolicking under its branches as the audience sat under its canopy. Snakes resting in the upper branches were apparently so bedazzled by the performance, they lost their grip and fell into the audience resulting in some of the most inspired and energetic choreography of the evening.

To find it, go south out of Charleston on US 17 (Savannah Highway) to Main Road and turn left. Look for signs to Kiawah and Seabrook Islands. After Main crosses Bohicket, it is exactly 7.3 miles to the sign marking the entrance to Angel Oak. The sandy road will look like a mistake, but stay with it, and it will take you to a sight well worth seeing. Best of all, it's free. Call (843) 559-3496 for more information and shop hours.

Spiritual Makeovers Done Here

Moncks Corner

We don't mean to suggest that your spirituality is lacking, but if you happen to need a tune-up, South Carolina has you covered. On a historic rice plantation, once the home of Revolutionary War patriot Henry Laurens, there is now a beautiful oasis called Mepkin Abbey. There, a stalwart band of monks lives, works, and prays in a religious compound they've occupied since 1949. Its setting on the quiet banks of the Cooper River first attracted publishing giant Henry Luce (*Time* and *Life* magazines), along with his diplomat wife, Claire Booth Luce, in the 1930s. Their winter retreat was designed by Edward Durell Stone and was a popular stop for many famous intelligentsia of that era.

In 1949 after the unexpected death of the Luces' daughter, the estate was transferred to the Roman Catholic Church and in turn, the monks of Gethsemani from Kentucky. This highly disciplined sect belongs to the Cistercian Order popularly known as Trappist. The monks dedicate their lives to study and prayer in the belief that entreating God for mercy benefits the whole world. And the way things are going, they're not a moment too soon. The monks were almost self-sufficient managing a commercial egg farm on the property, which supplied fresh eggs for sale in grocery stores all over the Lowcountry. This evoked the ire of PETA (People for the Ethical Treatment of Animals), who successfully closed the monks' operation. These days the product sold at Mepkin is strictly organic, mushrooms and garden compost that are slowly replacing the egg production business.

The atmosphere of Mepkin Abbey is contemplative and refreshing. Individuals with something to resolve internally may go to the abbey for a time of retreat and meditation by special arrangement in advance. Guests are expected to fit in with the rhythmic schedule of monastic life while there. Casual day visitors may check in with the guestmaster at the abbey's reception center and gift shop for tours of the chapel, library, and gardens. At Christmastime their display of crèches from all over the world attracts appreciative crowds and has become an annual pilgrimage for many families. Many retreatants leave Mepkin Abbey refreshed, renewed, and better persons for having been there. For directions and more visit www.mepkinabbey.org.

Tale of a Lighthouse Gone to Sea
Morris Island/Folly Beach

Somewhere in time the lighthouse stopped being just a navigational tool and became an icon of something more. Somehow it became a symbol for guidance and direction and a universal haven of safety from life's inevitable storms. Not surprisingly, a lighthouse in jeopardy evokes powerful emotions in those who have fallen under the spell of these brave and stalwart towers of comfort and emblems of survival. Just off the northeast corner of Folly Beach, near the eroding shore of Morris Island, stands the curious survivor of an entire lighthouse compound that once guided ships into Charleston Harbor. This lone survivor stands precariously surrounded by water in defiance of the sea itself.

The Morris Island Lighthouse was built in 1876 standing 174 feet tall with a state-of-the-art Fresnel lens that magnified its guiding light

The Morris Island Lighthouse is one of the most challenging preservation projects in the Lowcountry.

18¾ miles out to sea. In the decades after the Civil War, the harbor was deepened to accommodate larger ships in a Reconstruction economy. Protective jetties were built and caused a cascade of erosion to begin along the barrier islands surrounding Charleston, and Morris Island was directly in the path. Originally, the Morris Island Lighthouse stood on land twenty-seven hundred feet from the shoreline; by 1938, it was at water's edge. The lightkeeper's house was dismantled and moved ashore, other buildings were razed, and the light was automated, but nothing could turn back the encroaching tide. By 1956 plans were announced to replace the aging lighthouse itself with a modern, high-tech version on nearby Sullivan's Island. In 1962 the Morris Island Lighthouse was officially decommissioned, and its light went dark after eighty-six years of faithful service. The remainder of the island and the abandoned lighthouse passed through a number of owners' hands. For everyone the question was: What do you do about a lighthouse that was by now standing alone in the surf?

Up stepped a group of concerned lighthouse lovers who called themselves Save the Light, Inc. and raised funds to save this relic of Charleston's maritime past. Their appearance in the early days of the new twenty-first century seemed to come in the nick of time as by now the lighthouse was leaning slightly to the northeast under ever-shifting sands. Sophisticated engineering, impassioned dedication, and $8 million plus will be needed before the Morris Island Lighthouse can be called "saved," but this quintessential exercise in preservation, technology, maritime history, and flat-out romance continues on. To see the progress for yourself, take East Ashley Avenue on Folly Beach until it terminates in a small parking lot. Walk about a quarter mile to the northeast end of the beach to get the best view. Resist the temptation to wade farther as the shifting tides and currents in these waters are unpredictable. For more visit www.savethelight.org.

Publicity in a Trunk
Mount Pleasant

In the early 1950s the competition for viewers between Lowcountry television stations reached gigantic proportion in the form of a mascot named "Susie Q." She was an Asian elephant procured by NBC affiliate WUSN's owner, Drayton Hastie, to draw attention away from rival, WCSC (CBS affiliate), the city's premier broadcast station. And it almost worked. She lived onsite at the station's Mount Pleasant studios where travelers on Coleman Boulevard enjoyed seeing her on a daily basis. Children could visit her on field trips and family outings, and she made personal appearances at special events. The trouble with pachyderms is they are hard to contain, and occasionally Susie Q got loose and went trumpeting through the quiet neighborhoods of suburban Mount Pleasant, but that only added to her fame. Her greatest adventure may have been in 1958 when she was stolen by two Citadel

★ ★

cadets to make an appearance at a Bulldog football game in Johnson Hagood Stadium. Halfway across the old, roller-coaster-like Cooper River Bridge the trailer began to fishtail. Susie Q looked peaked, and the cadets wondered if they had bitten off more than they could chew. But she made it, and the prank eventually entered the realm of Citadel legend and lore.

After her career of celebrity, Susie Q retired to an animal sanctuary somewhere in Tennessee, and the days of one-upmanship competition between rival network affiliates have faded into distant memory, recalled only by the few old timers still remaining in today's cable-savvy world.

A Tisket, A Tasket, A Sweetgrass Basket
Mount Pleasant

If you are looking for a Lowcountry souvenir, you can't do better than to choose a sweetgrass basket. Think about it; they're light, easy to pack, unbreakable, authentic as it gets, and set off no alarms at the airport. And oh, yes, they are easy to find. They're sold on the sidewalks of downtown Charleston at the Four Corners of Law (Meeting and Broad Streets; see "The Center of the Universe?" page 15) and in the Market, as well as along the stretch of US 17 leading out of Mount Pleasant toward Georgetown. Don't be confused by the sidewalk displays or the ragtag, makeshift selling stands along the roadside: what's for sale here is fine art.

Don't be surprised if the vendors are weaving the baskets and tending their stalls at the same time. Each basket is a time-consuming project, and this craft has been handed down through generations, dating back to the days of slavery in the colonies. Although the skill is African, the materials couldn't be more typical of the Lowcountry itself. The baskets are made from bunches of sweetgrass, pine needles, and bulrush from the marsh tied together by strips of palmetto fronds. These materials are varied in their arrangement to create patterns that are utilitarian as well as beautiful. Traditionally, the men of the family

Choosing a sweetgrass basket to buy is
a joyful challenge for the eye.

gather the grasses, and the women weave and sell their wares. Like
many other artists some weavers are more highly skilled than others; in
other words, some basket weavers have become celebrities. Mary Jackson, for instance, has made sweetgrass creations that are now in the
Smithsonian collection, and her work is priced accordingly.

The baskets may seem expensive, but it helps to remember each
basket is unique. And you are helping to preserve a traditional art form
as quintessentially Lowcountry as shrimp and grits. Souvenirs come and
go, but a sweetgrass basket is a joy forever. For information on Mount
Pleasant's Sweetgrass Festival, call (843) 856-9732 or visit www.sweet
grassfestival.org.

★ ★

Charleston's Forensic Mystery
North Charleston

So far there's no TV show called *Charleston CSI,* but there ought to be. On August 8, 2000, the CSS *Hunley* broke the surface of the choppy Atlantic about four miles outside Charleston Harbor to complete a voyage begun 136 years earlier. In 1864 she was top secret technology and, in the last months of the Civil War, the first submarine in history to sink an enemy ship. On February 17, 1864, under the cover of night her crew hand cranked the propeller as she slipped beneath the surface toward the wooden-hulled, steam sloop USS *Housatonic* five and a half miles east-southeast of Fort Sumter. The *Hunley's* lethal sting was a barbed explosive device attached to a twenty-foot-long spar bolted to the sub's bow. She rammed the spar into the *Housatonic's*

History's homecoming postponed

hull affixing the explosive charge. She then backed away, pulling a trigger rope detonating 135 pounds of black powder amid a hail of retaliatory fire. In a violent explosion the *Housatonic* sank in minutes. Amazingly, only five Union lives were lost. Then, unaccountably, the *Hunley* vanished with her crew of eight Confederate volunteers and entered the realm of maritime legend forever.

The location of the *Hunley* and her crew were unknown until May 1995. Shipwreck hunters discovered it buried under three feet of silt on the seaward side of the *Housatonic*'s watery grave. After years of wrangling over state-of-the-art salvage technology, funding, and legal rights to the wreck, she was returned to the surface and the next phase of her mystery began.

Today she rests in a special research laboratory named the Warren Lasch Conservation Center in North Charleston, where slowly her secrets are stubbornly surrendering to forensic study. Was she disabled during her encounter with the *Housatonic?* Was another vessel somehow involved? Was it human or mechanical failure that cost her crew their lives? Still no one knows. The remains of the crew now rest with honors at Charleston's Magnolia Cemetery (see "Magnolia: Romance in Repose," page 27). And the world awaits definitive answers to the unsolved mystery of the ill-fated *Hunley* and her tragic crew.

To visit the conservation laboratory, call (877) 448-6539 or (843) 744-2186 for tickets and reservations for the guided tour. Also visit www.hunley.org for available tour times and directions.

Every Boy's Dream
North Charleston

It's a kind of alchemy; turn a bunch of little boys loose in a room full of bright red fire engines, and there's an inevitable explosion of pure joy. It has something to do with the excitement of fire itself mixed with a natural fixation on firemen and their bravery. Then mix in eighteen meticulously restored firefighting engines that trace the history and evolution of firefighting in general, and the stimulation is undeniable.

This scenario is played out every day at the North Charleston and American LaFrance Fire Museum and Educational Center. It takes so long to say the entire name of the museum you could almost squelch three or four fires in the time it takes to say it.

There's lots to see and plenty of room to see it in. The twenty-six-thousand-square-foot facility houses colonial era firefighting equipment from the 1780s through a 1973 Century Series Pumper manufactured by the American LaFrance Company, which owns and sponsors the $5 million collection. Many of the exhibits are interactive and hands-on, so little firefighter wannabes are free to explore and enjoy it all. The educational component of this museum is very strong. Fire prevention is emphasized both subtly and dramatically. A realistic simulator shows kids exactly what a firefighter sees as a fire truck races through the city. Blazing horns, vibrating seats, and flashing lights all make it seem real. Another exhibit traces the important decision-making required to successfully fight a house fire. Kids even learn how to slide down a fireman's pole, and how to exit a burning building safely. What more could a boy (or girl) want?

"A Rose by Any Other Name . . ."

Native-born South Carolinians and those so beguiled as to move to the state quickly learn one of the basic facts of life. Ridiculously big roaches have been here since time began, and they'll be here long after we're gone. People try to deal with them by using the term "Palmetto Bug," a more acceptable moniker, but the bottom line is: There are only two kinds of South Carolinians—those who have roaches and those who lie.

This is an ideal outing for families, school and church groups, or even adults whose hearts beat faster when a fire truck goes by en route to another dangerous rescue. It's located near the Tanger Outlet Mall at 4975 Centre Pointe Drive in North Charleston. Call (843) 740-5550 or visit www.legacyofheroes.org.

Osceola Loses His Head in South Carolina
Sullivan's Island

One of the more bizarre tourist sites in Charleston has to be the grave of nineteenth-century Native American warrior and Seminole leader Osceola on the grounds of Fort Moultrie on Sullivan's Island. As monuments go, it's not much more than a small plot of ground surrounded

Sad end for a proud man

by a wrought-iron fence with a modest marker. But then again, he's really not all there.

Osceola had nobly led his people in the bloody resistance known as the Second Seminole War of the 1830s, when the tribe fiercely fought against their forced relocation to the West. After two years of stalemate fighting in the Florida swamps, the U.S. Army and the Seminoles were coaxed into negotiations for peace under the guise of a white flag of truce.

Even though this meeting was one of the most familiar rules of military engagement, the breaking of which was considered uncivilized warfare, Osceola and his party were suddenly surrounded and shackled. Escape would have been futile as the Indians were greatly outnumbered. Still, this blatant betrayal of common decency shocked the general public at the time, and Osceola was the focus of sympathy in newspaper accounts published all over the country.

The warrior and 236 of his fellow prisoners of war were brought to South Carolina's Fort Moultrie in early 1838. By this time, his health was failing and medical attention by local doctors came too late. He died at age thirty-four and was given a military funeral with all the honors. Incredibly, the night before his burial, the attending physician removed Osceola's head from his body, and quietly returned the corpse to its coffin. The head, preserved in a jar of murky formaldehyde, turned up in several bizarre places over the years. It was displayed for a time in the window of a drugstore in St. Augustine, Florida. Later, it turned up in a New York medical college and is said to have been lost in a major fire there. Rumors abound of the head's miraculous survival and its being part of a private collection of oddities today. So rampant were the rumors of its whereabouts, and so frequently was the gravesite vandalized, that a full archaeological investigation was made in 1966 of the Fort Moultrie gravesite. Indeed, a headless skeleton was found and the remains identified as Osceola. The head has never been located.

As disrespectful and unjust as this treatment may seem, the man who was Osceola is nevertheless remembered in a national forest, a state park, and the names of several towns, counties, lakes, and mountains throughout his native land. His portrait (head completely intact) is on prominent display in the Smithsonian Institution in Washington, D.C.

To visit Fort Moultrie, cross the Ravenel Bridge (US 17 North) through Mount Pleasant to Sullivan's Island and turn right on Middle Street. Fort Moultrie is one and a half miles south on the left. Call (843) 883-3123 or visit www.nps.gov-fosu.

Palmetto Pride
Sullivan's Island

Do not call it a palm tree; that is a serious faux pas in South Carolina. It is now and forevermore a palmetto tree. It is not only on the state flag, it is also in the hearts and minds of all good South Carolinians.

Rows of palmetto trees line parade grounds, roads, and government buildings throughout South Carolina. Natives cherish it. Some know how to take the fronds and weave them into baskets and hats. At Christmastime, the fronds are an integral part of door wreaths.

South Carolina's palmetto trees have withstood multiple hurricanes, two major wars, and one devastating earthquake. But there was one calamity that makes our state tree very special.

When Charleston was under siege during the Revolution, the enterprising sons of our state who were defending it decided to cut and pile palmetto tree logs on the walls and ramparts of Fort Moultrie on Sullivan's Island. Fort Moultrie was put there to protect Charleston Harbor. If the fort's walls collapsed under the heavy cannon fire from the British ships, surely Charleston would fall. Would the palmetto logs work? And if so, for how long? There were huge explosions, crackling gunfire, and Fort Moultrie was covered in smoke from the assault. But when the breeze cleared the scene, the British were astounded to see that not only was the fort still standing, it appeared to be almost perfectly intact.

The tough, fibrous palmetto trees lining the fort's walls had withstood the best cannon fire that the British could muster. Essentially

★ ★

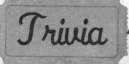

There's a sign at one of the marinas on Folly Beach that warns:
UNATTENDED CHILDREN WILL BE SOLD FOR BAIT.

the cannonballs bounced off the logs without harmful effect. Quite a few history books state that this action was one of the most important victories for the Patriot cause. The fort remained intact to continue its protection of Charleston Harbor, and the astonished Limeys needed to turn back north and replenish their cannonballs.

Fort Moultrie still stands today. The fort has been restored to portray its entire 171-year history (1776–1947) defending Charleston Harbor. From Charleston, take US 17 North through Mount Pleasant to Sullivan's Island, and turn right on Middle Street. The fort is about one and a half miles from the intersection. Drive out and take a look. For more information, visit www.nps.gov/fosu.

Just Your Cup of Tea
Wadmalaw Island

There's more to your breakfast cup of tea than meets the eye (or the lip as the case may be). Just how much goes into the making of tea is demonstrated at the Charleston Tea Plantation on Wadmalaw Island. A bit off the beaten track but well worth seeing is this fascinating, unexpected attraction featuring a processing plant, retail shop, and vast fields containing hundreds of thousands of tea plants (*Camellia sinensis*). Visitors follow the tender tea leaves being processed from harvest through packaging in a carefully controlled environment. This is an unusual tourist experience, but a unique one as this is America's only tea plantation.

It's all in the tea leaves.

Even though nature doesn't allow harvesting every day, the entire black tea manufacturing process is shown on three large screens displayed along the viewing gallery. Guests can sample tea and shop for distinctive teapots and other fine items in the pleasant Tea Shoppe. If you like you can take a relaxing ride through majestic live oaks to the fields on the Charleston Tea Plantation Trolley.

Cross the Ashley River Bridge (US 17 South) bearing left on Folly Road (SC 171) to Maybank Highway (SC 700) and turn right at the traffic light. Continue for eighteen miles on Maybank and look for the entrance signs on the left. Call (843) 559-0383 or visit www .charlestonteaplantation.com.

Talent Concentrate
Walterboro

A state as geographically diverse as South Carolina has an equally diverse cultural output of arts and crafts. Getting the best of the best together in one place is the mission of the South Carolina Artisans Center in Walterboro, only about forty miles from Charleston. The net result of this concentration is a gallery so rich in heritage and culture and so laden with talent and skill that you can practically touch, feel, taste, and hear the essence of South Carolina.

The whole idea for the center began in 1994 when two ladies from Walterboro and another from Columbia joined forces to found an arts center to display cooperatively the very best of the state's creative genius. The center is in a little village of historic houses that gives the art a quaint and natural setting for display indoors and out. Every artist goes through a strict juried process to ensure the work is of the highest standard possible. And thus, all the objects of clay, wood, glass, metal, fiber, and mixed media you'll see have won their right to be there. In 2000, the South Carolina legislature designated the center as the Official South Carolina Folk and Art Center.

Items are priced from a few dollars to several thousands. The collection is always changing, but some recent showings have included loomed shawls, hand-blown glass, ceramics, photography, watercolors, oil paintings, and handmade jewelry. Folks looking for South Carolina's indigenous sweetgrass baskets (see "A Tisket, A Tasket, A Sweetgrass Basket," page 62) and face jugs will not be disappointed. The third Saturday of every month a special hands-on demonstration called "Handmade: A Celebration of the Elements of Craft" features one artist in an in-depth person-to-person interaction with the audience.

It's an easy two-mile hop from I-95 to the South Carolina Artisans Center via exits 53 and 57. The address is 318 Wichman Street, Walterboro. Visit www.scartisancenter.com or call (843) 549-0011 for more.

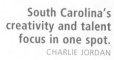

South Carolina's creativity and talent focus in one spot.
CHARLIE JORDAN

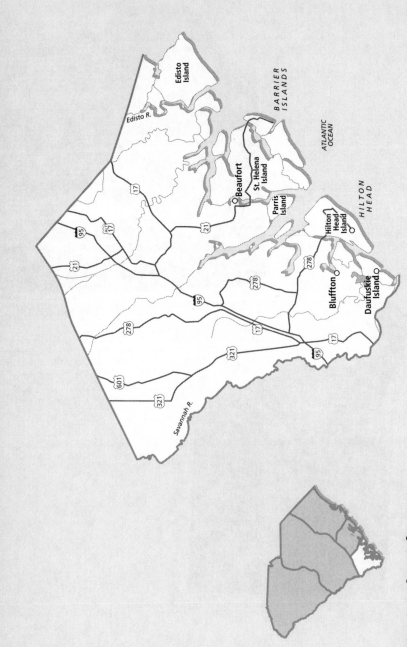

The Southern Corner

2

The Southern Corner

The hundred miles *or so that stretch from Charleston down to Savannah feature some of the best beaches in America. They're scattered along pristine barrier islands that not surprisingly have become upscale resorts, gated communities, and nationally ranked golf destinations. But a few miles inland the eccentricities of which South Carolina is proud flourish like scrub palmetto trees. From the pastoral beauty of the Old Sheldon Church ruins to the mystery of a reborn African village, the key word is diversity. The African-American experience from slavery through the Civil Rights Era is evident in a myriad of ways—from the Red Piano Too store that celebrates black culture to the charming lilt of the Gullah language, the ethnic roots here grow deep and strong.*

Beaufort is a beautifully preserved miniature Charleston with a slightly deeper Southern accent. U-boats from Nazi Germany sniffed around these waters during World War II but never made an overt attack. They must have been intimidated by the will of these survivors who have survived attack by the British, surrender to the Union, the rigors of Reconstruction, and most amazingly, the renaissance of new wealth.

This is a land of hunters and sportsmen of all kinds. There's even a museum for the reptiles and serpents that call this their home. Not surprisingly, movies are drawn to the area's natural beauty, and Hollywood is a frequent caller in these parts. Forrest Gump, Prince of Tides, The Big Chill, *and* Conrack *are only a few of the films with images enhanced by Southern Corner settings. Here are a few more eccentricities that you might like to capture on film yourself.*

★ ★

Digging Up Dirt on South Carolina

Allendale County

Since the 1930s archaeologists have believed that the earliest humans to inhabit the Americas were from Asia. The theory goes that these people crossed the Bering Strait after the last Ice Age and settled North America from Canada to Panama. Today they are called the Clovis people, and they left ample evidence in several locations that all indicates they were here thirteen thousand years ago.

But new research and archaeological analysis resulting from digs in Allendale County throw that whole theory into doubt. In 1998 Dr. Albert Goodyear from the University of South Carolina was digging a Clovis site called "Topper." He discovered evidence of human occupation on a level several meters below the Clovis artifacts and embedded in ancient plant material (easy to carbon date) were what appeared to be stone tools probably used for hunting. These stone points had a distinctive style, and the site indicates that this was an ancient quarry used as a gathering place for the stone material called chert. If authenticated these tools would prove a pre-Clovis occupation some two thousand to three thousand years earlier. In any case acceptance of this evidence would mean rewriting everything previously thought to be the true pre-history of North America. Dr. Goodyear's proof of authenticity comes from the carbon dating of the plant material, which makes Topper the earliest carbon-dated site in North America. But academic approval of such a radical deviation from accepted fact is hard to come by. It may be years before Goodyear's findings become mainstream and even longer before the written prehistory of the Americas accepts the Topper findings.

Meanwhile, the Topper Site continues to undergo archaeological investigation, and the public is invited to follow the progress on their website or in person. Visitors can actually participate in the dig for a week or more under special arrangement. Can you dig it? For further information, visit www.allendale-expedition.net.

★ ★

A Festival and Then Some
Beaufort

Years ago someone came up with a Chamber of Commerce catch phrase to describe Beaufort, South Carolina. This sleepy little coastal metropolis between Charleston and Savannah has been minding its own business since colonial days. The American Revolution and the

Concerts and parties on land, cruising and raft races on the water
SUE JARRETT,
WWW.SUEJARRETT.COM

★ ★

Civil War played through the town with little ill effect, so the promotional term they came up with was "Beautiful Beaufort By the Sea." Its historic architecture and glistening harbor right on Port Royal Sound indeed offer a delightful destination, but it was never a regular stop for the international jet set. Fifty years or so ago, it was decided the town of Beaufort ought to celebrate itself. The city fathers got together, and the Beaufort Water Festival was born.

Today this nine-day party is the most fun you can have with your clothes on. Every year, usually in July, the festival rolls out, and people from near and far come to join the fun. There is always an air show, skydivers, a water-skiing exhibition, fireworks, and the obligatory parade. Over the years they've added events like fishing and golf tournaments, arts and crafts shows, and a Commodore's Ball. The mandatory beauty pageant searches for and selects the Queen of the Sea Islands. After a week of frolic as the sun goes down on Saturday night, there is a street dance down by the Beaufort River, and it always

A Pinch of Advice

The gentle art of catching Lowcountry crabs is a rite of passage learned by every South Carolinian knee-high to old age. Using fine equipment is the key.

Tie a string to a chicken neck and leave it out in the hot sun for at least three days. When it is fully "ripe" (your nose will know), throw the darn thing in any creek or off a nearby dock. Nature does the rest. Be advised: Have a net handy as a painful pinch from a crab can ruin a good time.

features a nationally known headline act. In years past, country music's The Gatlin Brothers and Jake Owen have appeared, as well as the beach music group The Embers. There are always hundreds of boats, many rafted together in the river. It is South Carolina's largest floating cocktail party. Words do not do it justice. It's Beaufort's biggest blowout all summer. Go to the website of The Beaufort Water Festival and look at the photos—www.bftwaterfestival.com. You'll see a whole lotta fun goin' on.

Traces of Colonial Spain
Beaufort County

In the mid-sixteenth-century around 1560, Spanish colonials were a major presence in South Carolina, particularly in and around what we now call Beaufort County. Just like the American Indians, the influence of the Spanish has left a long-standing legacy, none more enchanting than the present-day Marsh Tacky.

The Spanish brought horses with them for transportation and for use in battle. When they left, for a reason long lost to history, a fair number of these horses were set free and abandoned. Incredibly they're still here, or at least their progeny are. They are called Marsh Tackies because the horses still favor the marsh as their home.

They tend toward a shaggy coat, mostly a deep brown in color. Their diet consists mostly of local grasses and wild berries. The Marsh Tackies are somewhat smaller than domestic horses. They travel and live in small herds of about fifteen members. Like most herd animals, they are led by a dominant stallion. They are not as shy as most wild creatures, but seeing one is thought by the locals to be a sign of good luck.

If you are lucky, you might glimpse one in and around the marsh. They are often spotted in several locations around Hilton Head and Beaufort, where the marshland covers tens of thousands of acres. The horses are also sometimes sighted on a small island in Port Royal Sound called Kashmir by the locals. They exist peacefully with some wild goats that gave the island its original name.

★ ★

There are several other islands off Port Royal Sound, none that is more idyllic than Pritchard's Island. It is breathtakingly beautiful and completely uninhabited. The only footprints on the beach will be from the occasional visitor who comes by boat—and those hoofprints left by the elusive Marsh Tackies. For more on the Marsh Tackies, visit the Carolina Marsh Tacky Association's website at www.marshtacky.org.

Trivia

The superlatives for which the Edisto River is known completely overlook the other quality it has—drop-dead beautiful.
PHOTO BY RICK BOLT

South Carolina's 206-mile Edisto River is the longest black water river in North America. For those picturing a river of ebony ooze or flowing ink—give it up. The "black" comes from the tannic acid, an earthy dye, leached into the water by uncounted miles of cypress trees and other organic vegetation—sorry about that.

The Water Is Still Wide
Daufuskie Island

Say it. Da-fuss-key. It is what the early-nineteenth-century slaves called it. Legend has it Daufuskie means "The First Key" . . . or the first barrier island out of Savannah. It is another Gullah word (see "Gullah: A Fading Sand of the Past," page 84) coined by the slaves who rode the *Island Packet,* a trading boat that plied the waters behind the islands two hundred years ago.

Daufuskie gained some unwelcome publicity when Southern author Pat Conroy wrote *The Water Is Wide* recounting his teaching experiences on the island. During the early 1800s it had been a working plantation producing superior Sea Island cotton, worth ten times more than cotton from other places. After the Civil War, the plantation was abandoned and became overgrown with native flora and fauna. The only inhabitants in the Conroy era were the progeny of the slaves who had been freed. Until Hilton Head began to be developed across Calibogue Sound, the source of survival for these indigenous folk was the sound and the river. The Daufuskie islanders who still speak Gullah became expert fishermen and oyster gatherers, supplying seafood and deviled crabs to the commercial dock in Bluffton.

When the newly rich began flocking to Hilton Head in the late 1960s, flashy boats became the "in" status symbol. Off Daufuskie's north end, close by the public dock is a huge sandbar that regularly captured some of these new boats. This, in turn, gave birth to a cottage industry, rescuing the Yankees who had run aground.

The Hilton Head development explosion migrated across the sound in the early '80s, spawning several golf courses, expensive homesites, and a first-rate ferry system. The largest development, Melrose, was unique at the time, because the developers sold memberships that, in theory, were marketable. There was also another development created on the south end of the island where supposedly a pirate uprising had once taken place, and it took the iconic name, "Bloody Point."

Why go there today? Daufuskie is unique: It still is accessible only by boat, there are no cars on the island, and the scenery is breathtaking.

The roads are perfect for golf carts, they are paved with oyster shells, and the native folks are glad to see you. Daufuskie Island guided tours of the undeveloped side of the island can be booked for couples or groups. Call toll free, (800) 686-6996, or visit www.outsidehiltonhead .com to schedule a Daufuskie Island History & Artisans tour.

You've Got Mail

Edisto

One of the most amazing revelations about The Old Post Office on Edisto Island is the fact that it is there at all. Edisto is many things—a classic beach town of the 1950s for one thing. But it's not really known as a haven of fine dining. The Old Post Office Restaurant may be its singular exception.

There may still be some magic to its location, because the old building has been a gathering place for islanders and transplants for many years, once a United States Post Office and at another time a general store carrying everything a weekender would need. Everybody seems to know where it is and be drawn there. Since the 1980s the building has housed a restaurant attracting a solid stream of loyal patrons to a unique setting.

Upon arrival you encounter the last vestige of its former life as a post office. One wall still holds the individual post office boxes that connected Edisto islanders with the outside world. Otherwise, the décor is upscale, reserved, and intimate. The menu is an array of Lowcountry specialties with a gourmet twist. Take the grits, for instance. Grits are not particularly gourmet per se except for when they are stone ground onsite and prepared with a sophisticated touch of a chef who knows Lowcountry cooking inside and out. So popular are these grits with customers that take-home packages of this manna from heaven have been sold under the "OPO" brand name as a souvenir of the evening.

Only the freshest sea island produce is served, and the same is true of the freshly caught seafood and choice meats. Guests enjoy a good selection of wines to accompany their meal. Service has the friendliness and hospitality of the island itself, and this is witnessed even at the meal's end when the bill is presented. A handsome postcard featuring a watercolor rendering of The Old Post Office Restaurant is their parting gesture and a fine remembrance of an evening well spent. Everybody loves to get mail.

Like all fine dining it tends to be pricey, but it's worth it, and remember, you're a heck of a long way from Savannah or Charleston. Go for it. You won't be sorry. The Old Post Office Restaurant is at 1442 Highway 174, Edisto Island. Call (843) 869-2339 or visit www .theoldpostofficerestaurant.com.

Slithering Serpents and Gaping Gators, Egad!
Edisto Island

Somewhat off the beaten path but very much in the realm of South Carolina curiosities is the Edisto Island Serpentarium. This facility has an indoor solarium and outdoor enclosures to give the public an up close and personal interaction with an amazing array of native reptiles as well as fascinating species from all over the world. The Serpentarium is the brainchild of two local brothers, Ted and Heyward Clamp, who spent a lifetime collecting snakes and other critters and sharing their knowledge with others. Inside, their collection of live venomous and non-venomous snakes are displayed in glass cases with handpainted backgrounds illustrating their native habitat. Outdoor displays simulate natural habitats where alligators, turtles, and lizards bask in the sun, feed, swim, and nest behind low-walled enclosures. In fact the habitat is so realistic, you may be surprised when a twig springs to life, or a log suddenly yawns with mighty jaws.

The friendly staff is well prepared to disarm the public's understandable reluctance about these close encounters. They are especially good at dispelling the myths and misconceptions that surround these enigmatic creatures, some of whom have been with us for millions of years. The Serpentarium occasionally offers visitors informative lectures

* *

War's Time Out

Hilton Head Island

What was maybe the largest gathering of baseball fans in the nine-teenth century wasn't in a park. It wasn't in the sports pages, on the radio, and it wasn't even televised on ESPN. It was a sandlot baseball game played on the island of Hilton Head, of all places, and get this—it was played before a massive gathering of ten thousand occupying Union troops and their Confederate prisoners.

One team was drawn from members of the 165th New York Volunteer Infantry, who opposed players from the 47th and 48th New York Infantry Regiments. And are you ready? Here's the best part. It happened in 1862 on Christmas Day. No one recorded the final score, but one thing is for sure—the New York Yankees won.

Ticket to Danger

Hilton Head Island

Unknown to most Americans, during World War II German U-boats were quite active off the coast of South Carolina, and several were actually sunk off the North Carolina coast. As a result several Nazi sailors were taken prisoner. Among the possessions found on one of the sailors was a movie ticket stub from a theater in Savannah. It had long been suspected that the enemy U-boats had to be getting diesel fuel from somewhere, and with this ticket stub they were able to connect the dots.

There was a known group of German sympathizers living in two South Carolina towns in the Midlands, ironically called Denmark and Norway. It appears that the subs would come in at night and surface to refuel and recharge their batteries in the May River behind Hilton Head Island.

The German sympathizers who delivered the diesel fuel likely launched their boats from what is now known as the Estill Beach Landing on the May River. To refill the tanks of the U-boats they would

★ ★

have to make several time-consuming trips back and forth from the landing transporting the fuel, so it was entirely probable that the subs lingered undetected behind Hilton Head for several days.

At that time, there were few residents living on Hilton Head. On a moonless night, a German U-boat would have been very nearly invisible. It is only logical to presume that during this lull, one or more of the sympathizers served as chauffeur for the Nazi sailors as they succumbed to the irresistible allure of Savannah's charms.

Interestingly enough, hidden underwater there is a sixty-foot hole in the mouth of the May River where it joins the Intracoastal Waterway. This was probably the deep spot the U-boats used. It has to be poetic justice that the locals call this Nazi hiding place, "The Shark Hole."

Lowcountry: A Quick Definition

Generally speaking "Lowcountry" is a term used to describe the lower third of the state. This land is physically low, very near sea level, and prone to swamps, marsh, maritime forests, and a myriad of shallow rivers and winding creeks. Over time this geographical description has broadened to include the ethnic characteristics associated with this region, and the cultural mores that have evolved here. As a result, Lowcountry is now almost a universal term of endearment for a people, a place, and a way of life.

"Monkey Island" Joins the War on Terror
Morgan Island

There's an island off the coast of South Carolina near Beaufort populated entirely by monkeys. People aren't allowed there unless they come with special written permission and trained personnel as guides. The fact that it is an *island* keeps the animals in and interlopers out, ensuring the monkeys' isolation. Morgan Island's inhabitants are several thousand rhesus macaques who live and breed there for the sole purpose of medical research.

Over thirty years ago a private biomedical company bought the four hundred–acre island and established the monkey colony as a for-profit business. Soon after, locals began to refer to it as "Monkey Island." Several years ago the state purchased the island and leased it to another medical research company that uses primates in their work. Not surprisingly the island drew the wrath of animal-rights activists, who nearly succeeded in shutting down the whole operation. Then, along came 9/11 and with it a renewed concern for the possibility of biochemical warfare and its devastating consequences. Almost overnight the nation had a dire need for "soldiers" to be in the vanguard of this new threat. Like canaries in the mine, these animals can and do test our defenses against agents like anthrax, smallpox, and viral enemies like swine flu, bird flu, and contagious diseases as yet unnamed. The animal welfare groups are still unhappy with the existence of Monkey Island, but, for now, they are accepting the sad realities of modern warfare and its potential for global consequences.

Tempting as it may be to visit Morgan Island for yourself, it remains off limits to the public. Boaters coming near the island encounter signs that read FEDERAL PROJECT, RESTRICTED ACCESS, NO TRESPASSING, and they really mean it. Onsite security measures notwithstanding, the animals—all six thousand or so of them—are wild, aggressive, and have sharp teeth. You don't want to go there. Strange as it may seem, these unlikely soldiers are on our side, and thank God they are.

★ ★

Not Paris, France, by a Long Shot
Parris Island

So you think you know Parris Island, South Carolina. If you're among the million or so men and women who have come and gone from Parris Island for military training, you have a certain right to your opinion,

Mementos from Parris Island's early days as a military training station are part of the museum's exhibits.
USMC PHOTO, COURTESY OF PARRIS ISLAND MUSEUM

Artifacts from Parris Island's earliest days as a Spanish settlement are also part of the museum's exhibits.
USMC PHOTO, COURTESY OF PARRIS ISLAND MUSEUM

be it pro or con. But the simple truth is Parris Island deserves another visit. On this one barrier island slightly north of Beaufort, virtually everything that has happened to South Carolina has played out in microcosm.

Parris Island was home to Native Americans for over four thousand years. It was colonized by the French at Charlesfort (1562–1563) and the Spanish at Santa Elena (1566–1587), who left traces of some of the earliest European footholds in the New World. Then came the British colonial period and the American Revolution. A plantation system developed and flourished here until the Civil War. Next came the chaos of Reconstruction, and after the Spanish-American War, it was decided a military training facility should be built on the island. And that may be where your memories of Parris Island come in.

The one place that interprets this amid all the military distractions and Marine Corps training facilities is the Parris Island Museum at the Marine Corps Recruit Depot. This ten-thousand-square-foot facility has exhibits recounting the local history of the island and Port Royal region, and another section dedicated to recruit training practices from 1915 to the present day. A third section salutes the "United States Marine Corps in Service" throughout our country's major conflicts and peacekeeping missions as a world superpower. The museum contains thousands of artifacts and other materials that bring to life the people and things that have been a part of the island's story. Forgive your drill instructor if you must (for his gung-ho enthusiasm) and give Parris Island another chance.

The public is welcome and admission is free, but access may be limited due to security conditions at the time. Visit www.parrisisland museum.com or call (843) 228-2951 for further details. The Parris Island Museum is at 111 Panama Street, Beaufort.

Call to Order
Robertville

Anybody who has ever struggled through a meeting where conflicting viewpoints prohibit swift resolution has most likely been rescued by *Robert's Rules of Order*. It is a kind of Bible of mutually-agreed-upon conduct for groups of people negotiating through a stormy sea of varying opinions. Most folks today know that *Robert's Rules* can effectively calm the waters and move agendas through an orderly process toward conclusion. What most people don't know, however, is that this collection of parliamentary procedures was compiled and later

Between these covers lies the difference between random chaos and civilized order.

published by a South Carolinian in 1876. His name was Henry Martyn Robert, born in 1837 on his grandfather's plantation near Robertville, South Carolina. This factoid may come in handy during a heated game of trivia or for winning a quick bet in a pool hall or schoolyard. It's true—just another feather in South Carolina's well-festooned cap.

Grits Done Right

When our Yankee friends show up from the North for the first time, they seem a mite unsettled when they become cognizant that South Carolinians often eat grits twice a day, breakfast and dinner. Y'all need to try some done right, and you will never go back to cream of wheat.

So do it right. None of that instant gooey stuff grocery chains try to peddle to the unknowing, great unwashed. Stone Ground. Got it?

Here is a tried and true way to prepare grits properly. Five cups of chicken broth to one cup of stone ground grits, simmer and stir occasionally for about thirty minutes. Salt and pepper to taste, and add a generous chunk of butter. When it starts to thicken, add heavy cream.

Now, you have one fine foundation for nutrition. Simmer some shrumps (that is what we call shrimp) just until they turn pink. Serve them on top of the grits with a little crumbled bacon and you will have something so good, it will keep you comatose for at least one hour.

In the not-too-distant past, a friend was entertaining the captain of a nuclear submarine and served this for dinner. The captain announced that he was going to take some with him on the next trip. Fifteen or so days later, the friend received a message to please ship some grits to Rota, Spain, to be picked up by the sub. Mission accomplished. One more set of Yankees converted.

Stalwart Survivor among the Oaks

Sheldon

Almost unbearably romantic are the historic ruins of Old Sheldon Church. Standing alone in the woods not far from Beaufort, here is an eerie reflection of the turbulent history of South Carolina from colonial times to the present day. Built as Prince William Parish Church by the Anglicans who settled here in the 1740s, this handsome church with its subtly tapered Tuscan columns was a classic example of the Greek style so beloved in its day. Planter families from throughout the area worshipped here in the heady days before the American Revolution.

British troops burned the structure in 1779, but the congregants rebuilt this house of worship from the surviving walls in 1826 and resumed services. Now called Old Sheldon Church of Prince William Parish, it continued to serve the community until January 1865. In that year the building was burned again when General Sherman's Union

Twice burned but still compelling

troops swept through the area on their infamous "March to the Sea." The walls withstood the flames once more, but the church was never rebuilt. The stately brick columns of the classical portico still stand tall and defiant against history and time as do the altar and walls with their graceful arched windows. Gravestones surrounding the church bear the names of parishioners from colonial times to the present, and these ruins attract quiet, respectful visitors from all over the world. Not surprisingly this peaceful setting has drawn worshippers to an annual

Where Do I Find Some Southern Cooking?

When folks show up from the Frozennorth (yes, it is one word), one of the things they always ask for is to be taken to "some place we can get some real Southern cooking" . . . bless their hearts, they just don't get it.

Real Southern food in South Carolina is many things. It is preparation and taste and ambience; it is specifically Bar B Que and okra soup. It is dinner by candlelight and is a "sit-on-the-ground supper" during family reunions. Some of your perception of Southern food is a natural byproduct of whether you are a "come heah" or a "ben heah." It is tradition. It is honesty . . . no tofu, and nothing frozen. Unsweetened tea is a sacrilege and a felony. "Just add water grits" will mean instant disbarment from both the Junior League and any other meaningful social circle.

If you get three South Carolinians together who are from different parts of the state, good grace and common decency dictates that one should not discuss Bar B Que sauce. The Upstate crowd tends to

✱ ✱

Easter service where an offering serves to maintain these ruins and their story in perpetuity. Most of the year this is a delightful place to take a picnic and celebrate the peace and serenity of this icon of survival.

Old Sheldon Church is located between Gardens Corner and Yemassee. Traveling from Beaufort on US 21 North, bear left at the intersection of US 17 at Gardens Corner. Continue past the stop sign for a quarter mile and turn right on Old Sheldon Church Road. Go about two miles, and the ruins are on the right.

favor ketchup-based sauce, but the Midlands bunch praises mustard-based. The Lowcountry folks tend toward a spicy vinegar-based sauce. And since we are on the subject, you need to understand that real South Carolinians' Bar B Que is also preparation. Whole hogs are slow smoked in a pit over smoldering hickory coals for the better part of one day, and the men who stay up all night tending the fire just might have an adult libation and tell the same fishing stories they told the last time they stayed up all night.

Then there's the food itself. Southern food can be a wonderful concoction of shrimp, corn, smoked sausage, and new potatoes in an iron pot cooked by the river late in the afternoon. It can also be an oyster roast with some McClellanville or Bluffton oysters (locals call them singles) with saltine crackers and a cold beer. Sometimes it's a fresh pork roast from a hog killin'. (There is no "g" in killin'.) It is bringing a casserole dish to a sit-on-the-ground supper at the church.

It is that intangible attribute one finds in the enjoyment of friends and family, and if you don't understand that fact, then bring some tofu with you to nibble on while the rest of us enjoy what we prepared.

Bridge over Troubled Waters
St. Helena Island

On a sea island near Beaufort in a Rousseau-like setting is an active, still viable icon of African-American history. The Penn School named for Pennsylvania's William Penn was actually one of the first schools established to educate newly freed slaves. The date was 1862, several

The Secret of Frogmore Stew

If you happen to have the good fortune to visit one of the better seafood restaurants in the Lowcountry (not one of the chains where the food tastes like warm cardboard), be sure and ask for some Frogmore Stew. In parts of Horry and Georgetown Counties, it is also known as Beaufort Stew.

South Carolinians, for hundreds of years, have been throwing big outdoor parties where you can find an oyster roast, a barbecue, or if you are really, really lucky, a Frogmore Stew. These kinds of parties usually start during the fall in the late afternoon with a cocktail hour while the host prepares this feast for the gods. The starting point is a great big iron pot with a wood fire underneath. The ingredients tend to vary by township but may include Andouille sausage, copious amounts of Old Bay seasoning, cloves, clam juice, tomato paste, red potatoes, chopped Vidalia onion, fresh corn on half cobs, and heaping mounds of freshly caught Lowcountry shrimp. The food is added to the boiling pot of water in stages. The shrimp are the last to go in, as they are done in only three minutes or less.

months before Lincoln's Emancipation Proclamation on January 1, 1863. The population this remarkable school served consisted of several thousand African Americans who had been abandoned on the Sea Islands during the Civil War. Two Northern missionaries, Laura Towne and Ellen Murray, arrived in 1862 to begin this work, which became known as The Port Royal Experiment. The two idealistic, highly

Neophytes are often surprised that Frogmore Stew is made from Lowcountry ingredients without a frog leg in sight.

This is properly served at sundown on layers of newspaper under an old live oak tree draped with Spanish moss. Pour yourself a smile, sit down to supper, and send your spirits into abject contentment.

dedicated women spent the next forty years of their lives refining their task to meet the needs of these disenfranchised, uneducated people.

By 1900 the mission of what was now called Penn Normal Industrial and Agricultural School had expanded beyond basic literacy. It included carpentry, cobbling, wheel-wrighting, blacksmithing, agricultural sciences, and teacher training to broaden its outreach and effectiveness. Penn-educated teachers spread throughout the Sea Islands taking with them the skills, tools, and enlightenment of education. The school closed in 1948 but evolved into the Penn Community Services Center, an agency of advocacy for the self-sufficient Sea Islanders, and that work continues today through festivals, conferences, and grassroots political initiatives.

At one point in the 1960s Dr. Martin Luther King Jr. and members of the Southern Christian Leadership Conference (SCLC) used the center as a retreat and training site for key strategies for the Civil Rights Movement including the famous 1963 March on Washington, D.C. The Penn Center today recalls that remarkable arc through history from slavery through the social change of the Civil Rights Movement. The fifty-acre historic campus is open to visitors and is used for retreats, family reunions, and weddings. The center sponsors the Annual Penn Center Heritage Days Celebration every November, and maintains the York W. Bailey Museum and Shop and the Laura M. Towne Archives and Library. Visit www.penncenter.com or call (843) 838-2432 for more.

Sea Island Sensory Overload
St. Helena Island

Possibly the most fascinating art gallery in the Southeast is just outside Beaufort on US 21 near the middle of St. Helena Island. The place is called the Red Piano Too, and it features a large selection of African-American artwork and works by Caucasian artists as well. Most of the work is from local sources, but all of it has distinctive color, design, energy, and flair. The gallery features periodic exhibits of regional

The entrance to Red Piano Too is a portal to ethnic creativity—and downright fun. Painting: *A Day's Catch* **by Allen Fireall.**
COURTESY OF RED PIANO TOO

artists that are so popular Red Piano Too has become something of a cultural center for the whole Beaufort population.

Even the old wooden building has ethnic roots. It was built as a grocery serving people on and around the old Corner Plantation. The building has been on the National Register of Historic Places for years. Its tall ceilings and large windows flood the gallery with light and create a feast for the eye. For example a Boston-born self-taught artist named Cassandra Gillens has relocated to Beaufort to express her love for the culture and heritage she sees here. Her portraits of Southern families and their slices of life warmly capture the Gullah/Geechee lifestyle. (See "Gullah: A Fading Sand of the Past," page 84.)

There's also Asher Robinson, a white man living on Pawley's Island whose mixed media representations of fish and turtles have whimsy

★ ★

and wide appeal. You'll also find postcards, prints, and carvings—all with a cultural slant. This is the place to go for a bible translated into Gullah. There's even a room dedicated to the books of Pat Conroy whose connection to Beaufort is known by his many fans from his popular books and/or movies (*The Water Is Wide, The Great Santini,* and *The Prince of Tides*).

The Red Piano Too is at 870 Sea Island Parkway, St. Helena Island. For more information, call (843) 838-2241 or visit www.redpianotoo.com.

Tasteful T-Shirts

Today's cool cats are always on the lookout for commemorative T-shirts to wear for special occasions (or for shock value at work). Should you find yourself either in Hilton Head or near Lake Murray, here are two T-shirts you can find that are bound to impress everyone at the bar and the powers that be on the job.

If you are in Hilton Head, go across the bridge on US 278 and follow the signs to downtown Bluffton. There are only two main drags, so take the one toward Savannah. On your right, stop at one of the mom and pop eateries called—are you ready for this—the "Squat & Gobble." Make no mistake, you are not here for the fine ambience; you're here to eat, so you can buy the T-shirt with a straight face.

On the north side of Lake Murray, drive up to Chapin. There is only one main drag, and you will see the sign on your left before you get to the post office. Another of those "meat 'n three's" is a place called "Fat Buddies." Of course, if you have the Squat & Gobble T-shirt, then you just have to get the Fat Buddies shirt as well to add two more one-of-a-kind keepers to your collection.

Out of Africa, into South Carolina

The Village of Oyotunji, Beaufort County

South Carolina is one of the few states in America that has its own version of a community that originated as a social experiment. Ours is a
Yoruban African village. The catch here may be that this one has actually declared its independence from the state, the nation, and the world
at large. It claims to be a country of its own, yet it is located near the
town of Sheldon in Beaufort County off US 21. (Only a colorful sign on
the highway indicates the turn into the wooded compound.)

The genesis of this community goes back to the early 1970s when
a professional dancer with the Katherine Dunham Dance Company
of Chicago and New York bought undeveloped property in Beaufort
County. He had a vision of recapturing the ethnic heritage and authentic West African Yoruba culture (originating in Nigeria). His name
was Walter Eugene King, but he adopted the sobriquet, "Efuntola

This way into another country

★ ★

Oseijeman Adefunmi," and later took fourteen wives and declared himself Oba (or king) of the village.

He established a religious order based on African teachings called the Yoruba Temple. The ten-acre compound included ten temples and a number of separate shrines. At its height more than two hundred followers called the settlement home and engaged in subsistence farming for their sustenance. But over the decades the numbers dwindled to fewer than fifty. This may have resulted from changing leadership and

Adjust Your Calendar

Neanderthals labeled seasons based on the demands of life. It was not until the Roman calendar defined the seasons of the year (spring, summer, fall, and winter) that the ball started rolling worldwide. Up North, folks accepted the mantra as is, but South Carolinians, always on the cusp of the times, began to rename the seasons to fit with the real pace of life. Our labels are based on how we live and our religions.

- Bowl Season. This kicks off the New Year as we religiously observe, worship, and bet on the New Year and hunt for tickets to the Peach Bowl.
- *Sports Illustrated* Bathing Suit Season. The first warm day in mid-February, the postman arrives with this coveted missive featuring beautifully arranged pulchritude. All mankind in South Carolina, past the age of twelve, reads and dissects this issue for at least four days. It is also the first day we can go outside.
- The Masters Season. Muslims go to Mecca; we go to Augusta for

the spartan living conditions of no electricity, running water, or other modern conveniences. South Carolina's heat, humidity, and plentiful supply of insects may also have taken a toll on their numbers. However, the core village still remains the hub of a scattered community of up to four hundred people who follow the Yoruba Temple religious practices. The status of their secession from the United States is unknown, but the drums and dancing of these would-be Africans continue to echo through a unique section of the South Carolina woodlands.

the same reason. The dogwoods and azaleas are in full bloom. We watch every shot, even during the Wednesday Par 3 Match. Folks from the blustery North are known to bring their pale bodies down for some sun and pimento cheese sandwiches.

- **Tomato Sandwich Season.** About the last week in June the first Johns Island Tomatoes arrive; and here is the secret. First chill the tomatoes. Peel 'em and slice 'em thick. Put some Duke's Mayonnaise on white bread, then add crisp lettuce, three slices of crisp, thick bacon, and thin-sliced Vidalia onions, and be prepared to experience pure heaven. If properly prepared, just before the last bite, you will note that mayonnaise and tomato juice are oozing down your fingers.
- **College Football Season.** This season starts about August 15 with the Kick-Off Classic and almost always features a South Carolina team on Thursday night.

Now you know. It is critically important to understand that one does not schedule weddings, childbirth, or funerals that might interfere with these hallowed South Carolina seasons.

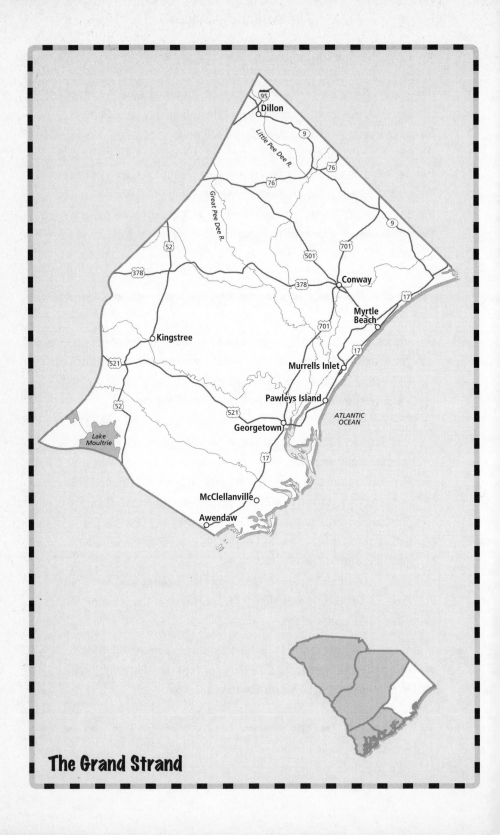

The Grand Strand

3

The Grand Strand

A hundred miles *or so north of Charleston you will find idyllic barrier islands, home to world-class golf resorts and upscale living. Then, the topography changes. Near Surfside, south of Myrtle Beach, the tides have created a broad sandy beach that is called "the Grand Strand." Here fishing shacks and summer homes have given way to high-rise condominiums and golf courses and an uber vacationland for Yankees and Canadians. The metamorphosis has been as complete as it has been extensive. People who haven't seen the area in a few years may not recognize it.*

Once away from the dazzling Grand Strand coastal waters another South Carolina emerges. For history lovers there's Georgetown, once the rice capital of the civilized world with that heritage celebrated in several unique ways. The small towns farther inland offer their own personalities for your approval. From the tiniest church near Conway to the over-the-top gaudiness of South of the Border, individualism is alive and well. From a Confederate monument wearing Union garb to the legend of the Gray Man who warns of hurricane disaster, there's always room for the odd man out. Where else would you look for an aquatic nature preserve named "Hell Hole Swamp"? The area has prehistoric shell rings where early man ate oysters in vast numbers for reasons lost to time. You can follow the exploits of Revolutionary War heroes and take shag lessons to the Big Band sound. It's all colorful, all fun to know or do, and it's all South Carolina. Just for you.

★ ★

Cravings of the Carnivores
Along the Coastal Plain of Northeastern South Carolina

If Carolina Bays (see "The Curious Carolina Bays," page 134) are a
macro phenomenon for South Carolina, then the tiny, rare, native
plant that grows among them is the micro example. The study of the
Venus flytrap (*Dionaea muscipula*) has benefited by the attention given
to Carolina Bays. In fact, the Venus flytrap is one of 630 species of
carnivorous plants known to exist on Earth. The largest of these meat-
eating plants are found in Malaysia and Australia and can actually capture and digest small rodents and reptiles. Our Southern native version,
however, has a more modest appetite. Its diminutive leaf pods slam
shut just like its larger cousins, but the menu consists of ants, katydids,
and the occasional bewildered beetle.

Feel free to abandon all fears of anything resembling "Audrey
Junior" from the 1960 movie *Little Shop of Horrors,* because the
Venus flytrap poses no threat to mankind. Mankind, on the other
hand, poses a considerable threat to the flytrap. The native habitat is
being diminished by development, deforestation, overuse of herbicides,
and poaching for commercial sales. But don't underestimate the tenacity of the Venus flytrap; it has no appetite for extinction. It stubbornly
hangs on in power line corridors, roadside ditches, and other places
that mock its natural wetland habitat. Beware all creepy crawlies; the
jaws of the Venus flytrap await.

Sky High Conservation
Awendaw

If you're a falcon with a broken talon, if you're a barred owl with a
torn wing, or if you're a red hawk who had an unhappy run-in with a
telephone wire, then you need a friend. In South Carolina that friend's
name is James D. Elliott Jr. He's executive director and founder of the
Avian Conservation Center dedicated to providing protection for avian
species and their habitat. Early in his career Elliott saw the urgent need
for professional care for injured birds of prey in South Carolina. He

Some residents of the Avian Center are temporary guests.
Others are full-time and play an educational role.
JOHN S. MEAD, WWW.BLUELIONPHOTOS.COM

established the Charleston Raptor Center as a medical clinic in his own home in 1991. As the natural habitats for these birds shrank against the encroachment of development, the need increased for avian care and rehabilitation services. Also emerging as a goal for the Center was education and advocacy for these unique species and their key role in our region's ecosystem. After Charleston attorney Joe Rice donated 152 acres near Awendaw for an enlarged facility, the Center's mission expanded to include The Center for Birds of Prey and The Avian Medical and Oiled Bird Treatment Facility. The umbrella over the entire organization became the nonprofit Avian Conservation Center in

2004. Also in 2004 construction was completed on eighteen display aviaries and a campus for additional educational purposes.

Today, visitors to the site can take a guided tour of the captive collection of more than forty species of birds of prey. Then guests can watch a flight demonstration by owls, eagles, hawks, falcons, and vultures over a flight field. Watching them soar and sail through the air is a lesson in their amazing hunting prowess and thrilling flying skills. The Countess Alicia Paolozzi Owl Wood provides visitors both day and night opportunities to watch owls from all over the world demonstrate their specific talents. Be forewarned: Your visit here may result in a life-changing appreciation for these magnificent birds of prey. For more information about tickets and directions, visit www.thecenterfor birdsofprey.org or call (843) 971-7474. The Avian Conservation Center is at 4872 Seewee Road in Awendaw.

The Biggest Oyster Roast Ever?
Awendaw

The time: roughly four thousand years ago. The place: the vast salt marsh surrounding what was later named Bull's Bay along coastal South Carolina. The people: nameless hunter-gatherers who predated the See Wee tribes who, in turn, greeted the first English settlers when they landed here in the late 1600s.

Exactly what happened on this site is somewhat of a mystery, but what is known without doubt is that these people used or ingested vast quantities of oysters, which were so abundant in surrounding creeks and estuaries that the supply was virtually endless. Over time these discarded shells piled up in a pattern that literally changed the landscape. Whether or not these oysters were consumed for sustenance or processed for some other purpose is still not clear. But the shell middens that remain after thousands of years of hurricanes, erosion, and natural decomposition still stand. The shell formation stands three to ten feet above grade and is mysteriously arranged in a ring with a diameter that measures up to 225 feet.

✶ ✶

Precisely what role the oyster played in the ceremonial life of these early people is unknown, but the sheer volume of this discarded material is certainly provocative and has led to several conflicting theories. Some archaeologists have said these oyster shells are what remained from some kind of fish trap; another theory is that these shells are remnants of foundations of structures long gone that were dwellings or ceremonial centers for the community. So stubborn is the mystery of who did this and why, even the name of this historic place, which is recognized and protected by the National Forest Service, is a misnomer. It's called the "See Wee Shell Ring," but carbon dating tells us it was there for eons before the See Wee arrived.

A mile-long trail and boardwalk with several interpretative stops winds through the site for those seeking a close-up and personal visit with the shell ring. To see it go to the Francis Marion National Forest on US 17. From Charleston go north of 17 to Doar Road (SC Route 432-S) and turn right. Go two and a half miles to Salt Pond Road and turn right on Forest Road 243. Go half a mile to the trailhead, which will be on your right. Visit www.fs.fed.us for more information.

And God Said, "Size Doesn't Matter"
Conway

No one can say South Carolina doesn't have a rich and diverse religious history. After all, the founders of the state came here in 1670 seeking religious freedom. This is where you find magnificent cathedrals and churches whose congregations have gathered together for hundreds of years. And this is where the countryside is scattered with quaint eighteenth-century (and earlier) chapels of ease that were built in the wilderness to ensure the Church of England's success in the colonies.

It was this spirit of taking the church to the people that played a role in the building of the Traveler's Chapel in 1972, which stands in Conway just northeast of Myrtle Beach along US 501 near the Waccamaw River. This twelve- by twenty-four-foot structure with only six pews and a seating capacity of twelve is known as "The Littlest Church in South Carolina." Some say it's one of the smallest churches in America. The intent was to serve the traveling public streaming to and from the distractions of Myrtle Beach, offering them a place to pray, rest, meditate, and gain inspiration. Coffers are fed by donations from passersby and the community-at-large which treasures its presence as a neighbor.

Early in its existence a storm heavily damaged the chapel, but it was rebuilt. Vandals broke in and set it on fire, but it rose again. Even the slings and arrows of recession and the excesses of bountiful times

Bye, Bye, Birdie

Like every other state South Carolina has a long list of official *somethings*. The state has an official state dog (Boykin Spaniel), and an official tree (Palmetto—surprise, surprise). There's a state insect (the praying mantis—no doubt an Episcopalian). There's even a state beverage (milk—yeah, sure). And of course the ever-popular state motto (*dum spiro, spero*—whatever that means). But nothing tops our official state bird (Carolina wren).

Was it ever thus? Of course not. We didn't have an official bird until the 1940s when it was deemed that our state bird would be the noisy mockingbird, but the state legislature felt the comparison to their orations was a cut too close to the bone. So revision was made in 1948, and its replacement was the feisty Carolina wren. Everyone in South Carolina has rested better ever since. We're grateful to the legislature for attending to this important matter and at last, giving us *the bird*.

have failed to impact the chapel's hold on the hearts of the people. Although no regular services are held here, almost a constant stream of weddings and commitment ceremonies take place under its roof.

No one denomination claims the church. It seems to be self-sustaining, and its size seems to endorse the biblical story of David and Goliath. Larger congregations should look hard at the strength and perseverance of the tiniest church in South Carolina.

The Traveler's Chapel is open twenty-four hours a day, seven days a week. It's located south of Conway, across from Coastal Carolina University on US 501 close to the intersection of Cox Ferry Road. Call (803) 504-1441 for more information.

"You Never Sausage a Place!" Sez Pedro
Dillon

The famous billboards are scattered throughout the state of South Carolina and reach as far as the borders of Virginia and Georgia. You can't miss them. The ads all feature in gaudy Day-Glo colors an iconic Mexican character named "Pedro." With increasing frequency as one drives closer to the South Carolina/North Carolina border, Pedro speaks in language that shatters all standards of political correctness and Pan-American good will. His message is always a coded invitation to stop and see South of the Border, an almost irresistible oasis of Mexican kitsch rising out of the hot Pee Dee clay beside I-95. With all the craziness, color, and chaos of the attractions, restaurants, accommodations, and souvenir venues, it's easy to overlook the fact that this is one of the most amazing marketing ploys ever accomplished on American soil. A 1930s hamburger/hot dog stand that also sold cold beer took advantage of the public's post-Prohibition appetite and found immediate success.

The whole enterprise was the brainchild of Alan Schafer, an entrepreneur and marketing wizard who died in 2001. At the peak of his empire there were more than 250 different billboards channeling weary travelers to enjoy a taste of Old Mexico in this unlikely setting.

★ ★

South of the Border's Pedro gets around.
PHOTO BY RICK BOLT

Even before arriving onsite families with children are excited by the specter of a giant Pedro looming ninety-seven feet into the sky, his feet planted eighteen feet deep in South Carolina soil. It's hard to resist the opportunity to drive through Pedro's bowed legs into an altered reality in the middle of nowhere. You might as well surrender and join the hundreds of thousands of others who have a pair of maracas or a straw sombrero proving you too went South of the Border in South Carolina.

Pedro sez to learn more veesit: www.thesouthoftheborder.com.

Stumpin' and Stompin'
Galivant's Ferry

Believe it or not there was a time in South Carolina when you could fire a shotgun in pretty much any direction and never hit a Republican. Every time elections came around the presumption was South Carolina would go Democratic. Even though the pendulum seems to have swung the other way in recent years, there is a bastion of "blue" from the old days that stubbornly lingers on. Welcome to Horry County's Galivant's Ferry Stump Meeting held every election year.

This tradition all began in 1876 when former Confederate general Wade Hampton rode into town on horseback and announced his bid for the governorship. He spoke at a place called "the Thicket" surrounded by admirers and voters of every stripe. Four years later, tobacco farmer and local businessman John W. Holliday, a man with political fire in his belly, successfully moved the meeting to his general store (a community gathering spot at the time). Democratic candidates have been speaking here on Holliday family land ever since.

In the early days speakers shared their ideas standing atop tree stumps to be heard above the crowd. This gave way to tabletops, wagons, and eventually stages. This gathering begat several similar political gatherings elsewhere in the county, but for some reason they've all petered out with the advent of modern campaigning through the broadcast, print, and social media. At the same time, however, the Galivant's Ferry Stump Meeting has gained momentum and importance, so that today it is one of the "must do" stops for any Democrat running for office—be it local, state, or national.

Political philosophy notwithstanding, this is also a darned good time. Attendees clog to country music and clap to gospel choirs. They drink cider (and who knows what else), and eat a concoction they call "chicken bog," a jambalaya-like dish with enough pepper to clear your sinuses. Politics in South Carolina is never dull, and the action is raucous enough for any party—Democratic or Republican. To learn more visit www.galivantsferrystump.com.

★ ★

History Slept Here
Georgetown

South Carolina is blessed with a number of fine, well run, working plantations. Hobcaw Barony, just off US 17 near Pawley's Island is just such a place. Not only is it beautiful as you might expect, but it also holds a cherished chapter of history. Steeped in beauty with hundreds

Funeralizing Down South

When a native dies in South Carolina, some believe that one does not really die in the usual sense, rather, "He's bought a ticket on the Big Bus." Of course it stands to reason that the cemetery becomes "The Big Bus."

There is a certain protocol that kicks in prior to the funeral. It is a well-orchestrated three- or four-day social occasion wherein the first thing that happens is that three or so ladies from the church show up and put the house in order, so that the family can receive visitors. Three or more ladies pitch in and fix about a dozen or so casseroles. On every squad, you can count on at least one lady that makes really good ham biscuits. The variations on this theme occur as a function of the family's religious affiliation. If they are Methodist, the food comes from a can. Presbyterians make it from scratch. Episcopalians open up a bar on the porch. Baptists go out to the garage to have a drink, so that the minister does not see them imbibing. Episcopal ministers usually drink more than anyone else.

of fine live oaks draped in Spanish moss, Hobcaw Barony was once the property of Bernard Baruch.

Mr. Baruch, a native of Camden and brilliant New York financier, was friends with the movers and shakers of the 1930s and 1940s. He hosted President Franklin D. Roosevelt and Prime Minister Winston Churchill and was known to be fond of the Bar B Que that the

The structure of the ceremony itself varies only slightly from funeral to funeral. One thing you can count on is singing all five verses of "Amazing Grace." If the family is Baptist, the preacher doesn't feel obligated to say too much about the deceasedp; rather he puts on about an hour of "soul saving." If he does say something about the departed, he tries to make it something good. There was the occasion a few years back when a particularly unpopular lawyer died in Charleston. He knew he was dying so being a lawyer, he decided to take no chances. He went to the Baptist minister in Mount Pleasant, saw the light, and gave the church copious amounts of money. The crowd at the church was abuzz before the service knowing full well that the deceased was a first rate jerk and could not wait to see what the minister would say that was positive. After the introit, the minister stood up, gripped the lectern with both hands, looked out over the congregation and said, "Alonzo Williams . . . was consistent!" The congregation breathed a sigh of relief and sat back in their pews.

A South Carolina send-off is more than a bus ride—it's a one-way ticket to a heavenly reward.

plantation hands fixed for him. Legend has it that D-Day was planned at Hobcaw Barony. No one alive today knows for sure whether or not that happened, but President Roosevelt, Mr. Churchill, and their staffs enjoyed an extended stay at Hobcaw Barony about the time when the invasion was planned.

There are many good stories to come out of Hobcaw Barony. One involved Mr. Baruch's daughter Belle. She was a striking lady standing

History and science co-exist at Hobcaw Barony.

six feet two inches tall and was quite regal. She excelled in every undertaking that struck her fancy, and she became a champion sailor and world-class horsewoman who won a number of international show jumping competitions. Like her father she had many interesting friends that came to call at Hobcaw Barony—among them Edith Wilson, wife of President Woodrow Wilson, whom she befriended during her work with the League of Nations, hoping to prevent future world wars.

Another story involves Mr. Baruch's last cook. His name was Yum Young. His specialty was Bar B Que. When Mr. Baruch's will was probated, it was discovered that he had left several acres of land on US 17, and sufficient funds for Yum Young to start a Bar B Que house. A young writer for *The State* newspaper named Bill McDonald was a regular customer. Bill had two talents; he was a wonderful writer, and he appreciated good "Que." Bill persuaded Yum Young to enter the first national Bar B Que contest in Washington. Good Que cooks from all over the country sent in their entries. Yum Young won the contest going away. In fact, he won the first three contests. His Bar B Que was so good, the other cooks did not have a chance, so he was retired from competition with an appropriate ceremony and given a handsome trophy in recognition of this feat.

Back at his restaurant, Yum Young was always present in his Sunday best, and the trophy had a prominent place on the mantel for all to see. Yum Young's Bar B Que got so famous that unless you walked in by four in the afternoon, you stood little chance of finding anything left. Yum Young's is long gone, but the memory of his Que gets told and retold at every tailgate and dove shoot in South Carolina.

At Belle's death, the Belle W. Baruch Foundation established Hobcaw Barony as a private 17,500-acre research reserve used by a number of the state's colleges and universities. The University of South Carolina and Clemson University have long-term research facilities there. To learn more about Hobcaw Barony or to schedule a tour, visit www.hobcawbarony.org.

★ ★

Who's on First?
Georgetown

The history books all record that the first permanent European settlements in the New World were St. Augustine (in Florida), founded in
1565, and the colony of Jamestown (in Virginia), founded in 1607.
South Carolina has its own claim to fame as settlements go. Lucas
Vasquez de Ayllon of Spain is known to have established a settlement
near Georgetown named San Miguel de Gualdape with six hundred
settlers in 1526. It was Europe's first inroad to the Americas even
though it lasted only a few months. Florida and Virginia are duly proud
of their colonial successes, but the effort made in South Carolina pre-
dates everybody else.

Rice Is Nice
Georgetown

Have you heard this one? "What do people in the Lowcountry and
people in China have in common? They worship their ancestors and
eat lots of rice."

But seriously, the real story of the rice culture of Georgetown
County is one of the most interesting and colorful chapters in South
Carolina's history. In fact, this may be true for the whole history of
American agriculture. It's all been captured here on Georgetown's
Front Street at the Rice Museum through fascinating maps, photo-
graphs, paintings, artifacts, and intricate dioramas. These exhibits take
the viewer on a complete journey of a rice crop from planting through
processing and eventual shipment to markets all over the world.

The Rice Museum is located in the Old Market Building, which
locals call "the town clock." This clock tower has become the architectural symbol of Georgetown, and this is a convenient place to review
booklets and tourist information about other points of interest and
attractions in Georgetown County.

Next door in the Kaminski Hardware Building, look for the exhibit
called "The Brown's Ferry Vessel." This archaeological exhibit displays

what remains of an early commercial river vessel that plied the waters of the Carolina coast during the early 1700s. Until its discovery, very little was known about South Carolina river vessels of this early period. This one was carrying a load of bricks when it sank near Brown's Ferry in about 1740. The site was excavated and the boat raised from its watery grave in a riverbank and meticulously preserved for this exhibit. What's left of its hull and keel illuminate a missing chapter in the Lowcountry's transportation history. The seventeen-minute video presentation called "Garden of Gold," is very worthwhile. It portrays the area's rice culture in an entertaining and easy-to-understand way. Admission to the next-door gallery, which features changing exhibits of local paintings, crafts, and sculpture relating to Georgetown, is free.

The Rice Museum is at 633 Front Street in downtown Georgetown. Call (843) 546-7423 or visit www.ricemuseum.org for details on hours and admission fees.

Once you visit you'll understand why rice appears on every restaurant's menu in the Lowcountry, and why they call it "Carolina Gold."

A Visit to The Sunset Lodge
Georgetown

One of the more entertaining, award-winning Broadway shows of a few decades ago was *The Best Little Whorehouse in Texas*. The play inspired a movie of the same title starring Burt Reynolds and Dolly Parton.

Texas had nothing on us since South Carolina had, perhaps, the most famous bordello on the East Coast, and it was still in business during the mid-'60s. The madame who ran Sunset Lodge in Georgetown was affectionately called "Miss Hazel" by her friends, who included the movers and shakers who wintered in the area each year. As the story goes, one of her most famous friends was a nationally known baseball magnate. Two of his considerable assets included the Boston Red Sox and several islands fronting the Atlantic Ocean just outside of Georgetown.

★ ★

Miss Hazel's establishment was generally left alone by the law for two reasons. First, it was well run and known to have many clients in the higher reaches of state government. The outsized political bloc in South Carolina of born again Christians left Miss Hazel alone as well, since she regularly gave monetary support to their political views. More importantly to Georgetown, Miss Hazel was known to be quite benevolent when the local Little League teams needed uniforms, or if some local church needed new stained-glass windows. Her baseball magnate friend was also quite benevolent. In fact, he left North Island, South Island, and most of Cat Island to the state in his will. Given the circumstances of this highly successful venture, it was thought to be a win/win for everybody.

Miss Hazel's "ladies" generally operated in New York until winter, at which time they tended to head toward Miami. The train stopped halfway between the two cities, and these ladies would work for Miss Hazel for a spell. Several had achieved a modicum of fame when they appeared as monthly fold-outs in *Nugget* and *Playboy*, two of the up and coming men's magazines of the era.

In a circuitous manner The Sunset Lodge provided college funds for one enterprising young cadet at The Citadel. It seems that he would raffle off a trip to The Sunset Lodge immediately after Saturday morning inspection to the freshman class for one dollar a chance. As soon as this young man had sold three hundred or so tickets, he would take the winner and buy him a quart of J. W. Dant at the Rutledge Avenue Liquor Store. After the winner was well oiled, the next stop was Andy's Steak House on Meeting Street in Charleston. Then, it was off to the Sunset.

There was one occasion wherein the winner turned out to be fresh out of his bar mitzvah before entering The Citadel, and, upon awakening from a colossal hangover and the trip to Georgetown, he became full of remorse for the dastardly deed in which he had participated and was overcome with guilt. It seems that this was his first trip away from home and out of the supervision of his overbearing mother. So he did

★ ★

what any young man would do under similar circumstances; he called his mother and confessed.

Of course, she was outraged and immediately called the Commandant of Cadets. She also spilled the name of the enterprising cadet who had organized the raffle. At The Citadel, when punishment is allocated, the worst is "Walking Tours." This means walking back and forth, with weapon and in a military manner, for not less than one hour. So, it came to pass that the raffle organizer was still walking tours right up until graduation.

A Good Time in Hell
Jamestown

Nobody ever accused South Carolinians of not making the best of a grim situation. Where else do you find people proud of a place they call Hell Hole Swamp, a haven for ravenous insects, writhing serpents, and reptiles with gaping jaws? So forbidding was this bog of dense, mossy cypress trees that even General Francis Marion, the "Swamp Fox," who retreated there during the American Revolution, called it "a hell of a hole." (See "Hunting for the Swamp Fox," page 206.) The name stuck and this primeval steam bath is a part of the Francis Marion National Forest, and people actually go there on purpose to celebrate the diverse wildlife and rich vegetation that flourishes there and seems untouched by mankind. The locals even started an annual festival in honor of this strange place that's been held since the early 1970s. Around the first week of May in the nearby village of Jamestown, they have organized a week-long series of backwater sports and down-home fun-making called the Hell Hole Swamp Festival.

The devilish name (see "The Devil's Playground," page 242) and the locale seem to encourage a certain kind of festival-goer whose interests are well served in this place. It features the 10K Gator Run, an Ugly Dog Contest, a best legs contest for women—and men, a spitting contest for kids, a contest among arm wrestlers and horseshow pitchers, and rides on a mechanical bull to see who can last longest.

The highlight of the festival week is the crowning of Miss Hell Hole, a coveted title and a ground-level entry to the sparkling Miss America crown. Sometime between the opening run and the closing fireworks you're liable to see celebrities in the crowd—one time (so far) there has been a visit by "Elvis" himself. To learn more visit www.festival-news.info and www.fs.fed.us/r8/fms/fmarion.

Kingstree's Stand-In for Honor
Kingstree

How could a monument to the noble sacrifice of the Confederate dead turn out to feature a soldier dressed in the distinctive uniform worn on the Union side? Not only could it happen, but it *did* happen in Kingstree, South Carolina, in Williamsburg County.

Back in May 1910, the local chapter of the United Daughters of the Confederacy (U.D.C.) and the respectful citizens of the county felt compelled to memorialize "the gallant band of volunteers from Williamsburg (County) whose courage, zeal and devotion fed the fires of patriotism that kept alive the flame during four years (1861–65) of arduous conflict. . . ."

The way to do this those days, of course, was to erect a statue in some prominent location lest the Civil War heritage and sacrifice ever be forgotten. Larger than life-size figures of heroes were usually carved by European artisans thousands of miles away from the South. So the funds were raised and an order was placed with a sculptor in Italy using the finest Italian marble.

The base however was ordered from the Southern Marble and Granite Company of Spartanburg, who promptly manufactured and delivered it to Kingstree. An official dedication ceremony was held despite the fact that the Confederate soldier intended to top the monument was still missing. A crowd of two thousand attended the event where city officials, visiting dignitaries, and representatives from the U.D.C. all gave orations. Everyone anticipated the arrival of a handsome representation of Confederate manhood in all his glory to take

The inappropriately dressed Confederate
soldier is oblivious to his faux pas.

his place on the lovingly prepared pedestal. Early-twentieth-century
production snafus, communication breakdowns, and sheer distance all
contributed to an atmosphere ripe for mistakes. Whatever really happened escaped the official public record, but the fact remains some
unholy switch was made. What was delivered to the Kingstree memorial site was a beautifully rendered marble soldier dressed in the unmis-
takable uniform of a Union soldier, holding his hat and rifle ready for
action. He still stands there today on the Williamsburg County Courthouse lawn. Subsequent investigations have uncovered a similar swap
occurred in York, Maine, wherein a Confederate soldier's likeness
stands memorializing the Union dead. But no definitive link has been
made between the two towns and their Italian suppliers, and the mystery remains unsolved to this day.

★ ★

What's in a Name?

Kingstree

When you start investigating the reasons South Carolina towns have some of the curious names they do, it can lead you down a fast road to serendipity. The town of Kingstree midway between Charleston and Florence is a prime example. Originally, the town was laid out in early colonial days by the Lords Proprietors, who were eight English noblemen who had received lands in the New World by the king's favor. They intended to found a town to be named in honor of King William of Orange (1650–1702). The name stuck for the county, which was called Williamsburg County, but the town itself succumbed to

The King's mighty tree is long gone but not forgotten.

another name entirely. It seems that near the planned town site was a giant white pine tree growing on the bank of the Black River. So tall and straight was this magnificent tree that it was marked with the king's broad arrow (badge of ownership) to reserve it for the mast of a future sailing vessel for the royal fleet. The king never received the ship's mast according to the story, but the town that grew up where "The King's Tree" stood has been called "Kingstree" ever since.

Miracle on King's Highway

McClellanville

Alone in the back wilderness of the Lowcountry outside of Georgetown sits a small but precious architectural treasure that dates from about 1768. This unlikely discovery in this rural setting is almost disorienting. But it makes an eloquent testimony to the power and importance of religion in colonial South Carolina. This Anglican parish was made up of area plantation owners whose wealth and political power were of great interest to the Church of England. Thus, churches like this were built in the hinterlands to make it "easy" for parishioners to worship and tithe. These satellite churches were called "chapels of ease."

Amazingly, several of these churches have survived, but none is more haunting and authentic than St. James-Santee in this unusual and unexpected setting. The church itself has two classical porticos each supported by four brick Doric columns. If you're lucky, the church may be open, and you can see the high-backed, boxed pews separated by a cross axis of clay tile flooring. The pews have never been painted. Only the pulpit is a modern replacement, and the general ambience of this little chapel is overwhelmingly romantic. St. James-Santee Church seems to generate its own will to survive. During the Civil War the chapel's communion silver was stolen, but after the war it was quietly returned. Vandals and vagrants have come and gone, but by some miracle, the building looks very much the same today as it did when it was the center of religious thought for the plantation families living on the Santee Delta. Even the road to get there (once known as the King's Highway) is a sandy path that is nearly impassable in rainy weather. The entire landscape seems arrested in time.

To find the church from Charleston, drive north on US 17 toward Georgetown. Turn left on SC 857 (Rutledge Road). After passing Hampton Plantation State Park on the right, travel another mile and turn left on the sandy road. St. James-Santee Church will be on the right. (While you're in the area, don't miss nearby Hampton Plantation; see "Our Boy George.") Visit www.stjamesec.org for more information.

Our Boy George
McClellanville

For most of us the image of George Washington is rather static. He's either crossing the frozen Delaware with his hand pointing majestically toward something, or he's looking down on us from his portrait frame in the classroom.

Here in South Carolina he's a friend of ours. He's been here, you see. He spent a lot of time here in 1791, and every night after he got off his horse they hung out a WASHINGTON SLEPT HERE sign.

Up in the Santee Delta on a beautiful plantation called Hampton, he paid a call for breakfast. Now, when the new president of the United States is coming for breakfast, you want to have your ducks in a row. The plantation house was spiffed up with a new coat of paint and, best of all, a handsome portico with four big columns was built expressly for the occasion. It was finished just in the nick of time.

When the president finally arrived, all the neighbors seemed to show up too. And everyone was dressed to the nines. The ladies adorned their dresses with sashes and bandeaux hand-painted with likenesses of the president's countenance.

The hosts and the presidential party were standing on the portico after breakfast, when the subject came up about a young live oak sprout in front of the house. The question was: Should the tree stay and be allowed to grow up or should it go? Washington had an opinion, which was let the oak grow. In those days, nobody argued with George.

Today, South Carolina youngsters (and everyone else) can visit Hampton Plantation and not only see what remains of Washington's tree, they can touch it. Yes, it's still alive! For those who'd actually like to make the connection with George's old tree, be advised Hampton Plantation takes a while to find. If you are coming from Charleston take US 17 North to McClellanville. It's located at 1950 Rutledge Road, McClellanville. (While you're in the vicinity, stop by St. James-Santee Church; see "Miracle on King's Highway," page 125.) For more information call (843) 546-9361 or visit www.southcarolinaparks.com.

Take a Second Look
Murrells Inlet

Travelers driving south on US 17 from Myrtle Beach toward Georgetown often do a double-take. On the right side of the road across from Huntington Beach State Park, they see two giant silver stallions atop a pedestal engaged in a ferocious battle. Actually, the horses are aluminum, not silver, the fighting is an artful battle frozen in sculpture, and this is only the beginning of what lies inside Brookgreen Gardens.

Brookgreen Gardens is the combination of four eighteenth- and nineteenth-century plantations: the Oaks, Springfield, Laurel Hill, and (old) Brookgreen. But since the late 1920s, crop-growing has hardly been the primary activity here. Instead, visitors now discover beautifully landscaped gardens sprawling over 350 acres of the property. Carefully posed within this perfectly groomed garden are five hundred pieces of outdoor sculpture—all created by renowned nineteenth- and twentieth-century American artists.

The vision of Brookgreen Gardens came from noted American sculptor Anna Hyatt Huntington, and her husband, philanthropist Archer M. Huntington. Back in the 1930s they created what came to be an outdoor sculpture museum to share with the public. Today the property is managed by a private organization, Brookgreen Gardens,

No animal is off-limits for capturing in Brookgreen's
fanciful sculpture garden.
EAT MORE BEEF BY SANDY SCOTT, COURTESY OF BROOKGREEN GARDENS

The *Fighting Stallions* at the entrance to Brookgreen are
only a teaser for all the stunning sculpture within.
FIGHTING STALLIONS BY ANNA HYATT HUNTINGTON,
COURTESY OF BROOKGREEN GARDENS

a Society for the Southeastern Flora and Fauna. Guests get an initial orientation at the visitors' pavilion for an overview of Brookgreen's diversity. Many choose to wander the seemingly endless paths and encounter the breathtaking sculpture individually. There's also a nature area where wildlife native to this part of South Carolina are housed and viewable in natural settings. If you're lucky, and you catch it at the right time (from mid-March through the end of November), you can take their tour boat and view the gardens as you glide through the swamp waters and estuaries. For those who want to experience Brookgreen Gardens even more intensely, a custom vehicle offers over-land excursions.

Brookgreen Gardens is located at 1931 Brookgreen Drive in Murrells Inlet. For more information about tickets and hours, call (843) 235-6000 or visit www.brookgreen.com.

Seafood and More for All Salty Dogs
Myrtle Beach

The name tries to say it all. It's called The Original Benjamin's Calabash Seafood and Nautical Museum, but that's only part of the story. For starters, "calabash" refers to a geographical region along the North Carolina/South Carolina coast and is not a flavoring, a spice, or a particular cooking method. Rather, it has to do with plenty of fresh, local seafood, Southern hospitality, and unbridled enthusiasm for all things from the sea. Many restaurants use the term and offer a fine meal, but this one claims to be the largest calabash seafood buffet in the world.

In addition to a 170-item buffet that serves up to five hundred guests at a time, there's a unique atmosphere that adds interest for anyone fascinated by the sea. Each of the nine dining rooms displays remarkable ship models of a different class of seagoing vessels, ranging from majestic ocean liners to world-class racing yachts. For instance, there's a thirty-foot model of HMS *Queen Elizabeth* that was presented to England's monarch before the ship was launched. There's

(Continued on Page 132)

It's Only a Game

As Yogi Berra might say, "Golf is 90 percent mental, the other half is skill." Mark Twain referred to golf as, "a good walk spoiled." In South Carolina, it can get more than a little crazy at times.

We have several real golf jewels in South Carolina. Quite a few golf courses rank very high in international rankings, including Harbor Town and Long Cove, both on Hilton Head Island. The Palmetto Club in Aiken has attracted a highly prominent national membership. It is worth the trip, if you can finagle your way to play there. Thankfully, not much has changed since the 1920s. In fact the road to the club is only partially paved, because Aiken is also horse country, and many of the residents still ride horseback through portions of the city. (See "Horsing Around in Aiken," page 145.) The men's locker room is paneled in the original tongue and groove heart pine with a potbellied stove for cool days. There is a framed letter on the wall sent by Roy Sears (as in Sears Department Stores) protesting the recent dues increase of $20 a year.

In Greenville, one of the better courses is Chanticleer. It is long and hard. Once a year they have "Tough Day" wherein they make it as hard as possible to survive eighteen holes. One year in the '80s, the wind blew quite hard on Tough Day, and no one broke eighty. Myrtle Beach has more than one hundred courses, which has transformed the area from just a summer vacation stop to a year-round golf-a-rama. The Canadians who play there, for instance, think that a forty-degree day in February is a short-sleeved day.

Just outside of Charleston is a fairly new course named Bull's Bay. The owner, a lawyer who made a fortune in the tobacco settlement cases, had more than a million cubic yards of soil moved to sculpt a rolling, championship course. In fact, the clubhouse sits up on a

The gallery fans of your golf game aren't all on the fairway.
PHOTO BY RICK BOLT

little mountain that was created just for that purpose. The Member/ Guest Tournament has become quite an event. There is a Calcutta (auction of player teams) that is always fueled by alcohol, but all of that takes second place to the bull event. The owner has a live bull staked out on a fairly long tether. His temporary pasture is marked off in squares, and each square is numbered. The participants then purchase the squares. Sometime during the tournament weekend nature takes its course, and the bull "votes." The guest who owns that square takes the prize. Is this a great country, or what?

(Continued from Page 129)

also a thirty-five-foot model of the *Mayflower* built for the 1952 Academy Award–winning film, *Plymouth Adventure,* starring Spencer Tracy and Lloyd Bridges. You'll also find an expert model builder on staff so patrons can observe new additions to the exhibit underway. As a homage to the sea itself, the restaurant has a dry sea aquarium with mounted specimens of every stripe as well as an eight hundred–gallon aquarium where tropical fish, eels, and sharks swim about for the enjoyment of customers.

In total this calabash adventure is sure to satisfy any taste. It is located at 9593 North King's Highway (US 17), a quarter mile north of Carolina Opry and three miles south of Barefoot Landing in Myrtle Beach. Call (800) 288-8687 or see www.originalbenjamins.com for more.

Dancefloor Devilment or Just Plain Fun?
Myrtle Beach

The Shag. In South Carolina, it is both a noun and a verb, because it is a dance. More importantly, it was the very best mating ritual ever invented by man or beast. For most South Carolinians of a certain age, it was a coming out ritual that far surpassed any debutante party. It was a way for both genders to connect.

Its roots go back to the late '50s on Myrtle Beach's Ocean Drive. There was a joint down on the beach that was little more than a concrete pad, a jukebox, and a frame made out of cull lumber. The jukebox was loaded with what came to be known as Motown music. Part of the ritual was a dress code for men that required madras Bermuda shorts, golf shirt, and Weejuns with no socks. For the uninitiated, Weejuns are penny loafers. Girls wore Bermuda shorts also and big hair . . . really, really big hair. Of course the girls were on one side and boys on the other. All of this was right across the street from the beach, which enabled girls who were being chaperoned to announce they were

★ ★

Shag's basic uniform. Now all he needs is a beach.

going to walk on the beach. Pabst Blue Ribbon was 50 cents, and there was a correct way to hold it, dangling down while you danced.

The joint jumped. It was that really good hard driving, thumping Motown with a two/four beat that just grabbed your soul and made you want to dance. From noon every day till the wee hours of the morning, the dance floor was packed. Songs were six for a quarter: Fats Domino, The Drifters, The Coasters, all black singers that our parents forbade us to listen to at home. If they only knew. . . .

And then about every sixth or tenth song, the jukebox played something slow . . . "The Great Pretender" or "Smoke Gets In Your Eyes." Then we danced up close, really close. The Baptist Church rose up in arms about this decadent dancing that was clearly the "work of the devil." We called it "belly rubbin.'"

Of course, other joints sprang up on the coast, such as the Folly Beach Pier House and a joint at Pawley's Island called The Pavilion that sat out over the marsh on stilts. It had a wooden floor and shutter holes for windows. When one of the chaperones wandered in one Saturday night and saw young people dancing really close after shagging for a few minutes, she was appalled. She left in a huff, and came back about an hour later with the Baptist minister in tow. Not only were they Baptists, they were *Deep Water* Baptists, so they fell on the floor and began to pray for the souls of the heathens. The crowd's response was to turn up the volume on the jukebox.

In fact this brouhaha only served to make the Shag more popular. When the good mamas of South Carolina told their children that the ministers had proclaimed the Shag an "evil act," everyone knew that this was something special. And, believe it or not, it is still running wide open. Every spring and every fall, there is an "SOS" party (Society of Stranders as in The Grand Strand) that runs for a whole week. It's centered at Ocean Drive and attracts fifty thousand or so folks, some still wearing Weejuns and madras shorts. Here's a tip. If you are from the North, it's a good idea to watch a while before you join the party. The Shag can be dangerous when done cold sober.

The Curious Carolina Bays
West of Myrtle Beach

At the depth of America's Depression in the 1930s, nature added insult to injury with a drought of unprecedented severity. The result was the infamous Dust Bowl, when millions of acres of fertile Midwestern cropland swirled into the sky in a barrage of dust storms dashing the dreams of thousands of farm families in an already stressful

★ ★

decade. Strangely, it was the government's effort to study the causes and measure the scope of that disaster that revealed a modern geological mystery that has yet to be solved.

Aerial photography had proved helpful during World War I in identifying enemy targets; now it was being used for soil and water conservation purposes. It was only when these photographs were pieced together in a mosaic portrait of the areas west of Myrtle Beach that a heretofore unknown anomaly was discovered. Strewn over the landscape were previously unnoticed oval-shaped irregularities in the earth—some filled with stands of trees, others disguised by swamps, lakes, and tall grasses. Scientists dubbed them "Carolina Bays"

No-See-Ums: Adding Insult to Injury

South Carolina in the full bloom of spring draws millions of visitors from all over the world who are attracted to its natural beauty, coastal pleasures, and architectural wonders. But that's not all it attracts. Springtime also brings forth the annual invasion of swarms of tiny flying insects called by locals, "no-see-ums." These minute vampires are so small they almost attain invisibility, but they require the protein of blood to breed and feed the next generation. And this is something they do with great success. All kinds of unguents, sprays, creams, powders, and goop have promised relief from these little devils, but nothing really works. Your only hope is for a gentle breeze to come along and blow them end over teacup into the next garden party, or better yet, the next state.

because of the bay trees that dominate the area. For many decades the experts debated as to the origins of these curious pockmarks in the earth. Theories range from strikes by swarms of meteorites to the wallowings of prehistoric whales. Others say they came from peat bog fires or melting glaciers. Nobody really knows.

Subsequent research has revealed as many as half a million other bays along the Eastern Seaboard, but the richest concentration is right here in South Carolina. Additional theories are always welcome. Go figure.

Heed the Gray Man
Pawley's Island

South Carolina has never been starved for fascinating ghost tales. Historical colonial cities like Beaufort, Charleston, and Georgetown are rife with colorful examples of every ilk from swashbuckling pirates to patriots and statesmen, from dashing young rebels and their star-crossed lovers to grieving parents separated from their children by illness and the accidents of fate. The common denominator seems to be mystery and romance. One tale stands out among the all the others: the legend of the Gray Man, whose ghostly appearance warns residents of Pawley's Island of impending danger come hurricane season.

The legend goes back to the early nineteenth century in various versions, but the point is always the same. The mysterious Gray Man is seen walking along the beach on Pawley's Island, a solitary figure cloaked in gray, who disappears when anyone approaches. He only makes a showing before a major hurricane strikes the local coast. Supposedly those who heed his warning and evacuate the island are spared the storm's terrible wrath. But those who ignore him experience the full force of the storm's fury and live to regret their rejection of the Gray Man's fair warning. The odd thing about the Gray Man seems to be his endurance through modern weather forecasting and even Doppler radar technology. As anyone who lives along the South Carolina coast knows, the hurricanes that make landfall can be devastating and leave scars that last for years, but residents also know hurricanes that only threaten the coast can be traumatizing as well. The threat can be almost as bad as the reality. Everyone hates the traffic jams, the hoarding of food and supplies, the interruption to business and leisure—all of which take a heavy toll.

The Gray Man seems to be batting a thousand on knowing the difference between those storms that are destined to strike and those that only frighten and turn away. He always seems to show up when the real thing is on its way, and residents of Pawley's Island and the whole South Carolina coast look for him whenever the skies turn an ominous gray.

Hammock Haven on Pawley's Island
Pawley's Island

Nestled between Myrtle Beach and Georgetown is a sleepy, old fishing village called Pawley's Island. Not so long ago it was a small colony of beach houses and mom and pop businesses along US 17, which skirts the state's coastline. One of these roadside compounds holds the distinction of being the "home of the Original Pawley's Island Rope Hammock." People come from far and wide looking to buy one of these hand-woven hammocks that have appealed to homeowners, sailors, and porch dwellers since 1889, when US 17 was just a dusty path.

The hammock was the brainchild of Captain Joshua John Ward, who operated a riverboat that ferried rice from the inland plantations to the wharves in Georgetown. Like all experienced sailors of his day, he was skillful at tying knots that would not shift, tangle, or fray in heavy use. Besides, he was tired of the hot, lumpy grass mattresses used on boats at the time. Captain Ward came up with his cooler, lighter hammock design made of white cotton rope to better cope with the sweltering, subtropical Carolina nights. Before long he found himself tying these hammocks for envious friends who admired his work.

Over a hundred years later that same Pawley's Island Rope Hammock is delighting visitors to the area and new residents who

**Hammocks don't come with instructions.
Their enjoyment comes naturally.**

appreciate a deliciously restful siesta and a refreshing sea breeze.
Today's hammock is an exact replica of the original and is being
shipped all over the world to appreciative audiences who know a good
thing when they sleep on it. All you need is a lemonade to sip and a
thick, engaging novel, and you're set to go.

Pick one up at The Original Hammock Shop at 10880 Ocean Highway on Pawley's Island, or call (800) 332-3490 or visit http://hammock
shop.com to order your very own.

★ ★

Cooper's Country Store Is a Real Time Tripper
Salters

If you are heading down mid-state toward Myrtle Beach, go a few minutes out of the way and drive down US 521. After you pass Salters, at the next cross road, SC 377, you will find an absolutely delightful throwback in time, Cooper's Country Store. Whatever you need, somewhere in the store they will have it.

The homemade sausage is to die for, and do not leave without some Bar B Que (pork, chicken, or turkey) skillfully cooked out back with a secret sauce. You'll find bream poles, crickets (in the big wooden box by the front door), worms, cast iron cookware, horse collars, nails, tools, pipe, buckshot, parts for your pump, slab bacon, streak-of-lean, mousetraps, and some really fine stone ground grits.

Crickets, sold for bait, chirp a welcome at the store's front door.

★ ★

There are $4 "grab bags," pork skins, and candy for the children. There is one item you cannot find up North, but if you really, really want to sample some South Carolina food, they will sell you some salt-cured country ham. Rumor has it that they use it in the operating room of the hospital in Florence to bring people back to life.

Mr. Theron Burrows opened the store in 1937 when gas was ten cents a gallon and a gallon of milk went for fifty cents. He died in 2003, and the business was taken over by a nephew, Russell Cooper.

Weather Report

Winter in South Carolina is something of a touchy subject. Generally speaking, we don't like to admit that we have winter at all. The lawyers on Broad Street in Charleston walk up and down the street in their blue blazers and khaki pants when there are faint but undeniable snowflakes in the air. Golfers are the same way. Players in pastel pants squint to find their shots when the morning dew is white with frost.

The summer weather here is also unique for several reasons. First of all the air is so thick you can not only feel it—you can see it. The humidity is measured in tons per square foot, and then there's the heat. Noontime in South Carolina is called "the heat of the day." When Northerners encounter the heat of the day for the first time, they often flinch. It takes some getting used to. Old timers and Southerners soon learn how to cope with the weather; they've learned the thing to do about it is to simply s-l-o-w down.

★ ★

Trivia

When playing golf on any coastal Carolina links, you may discover you're sharing the course with an alligator. The unofficial rule is: Let the gator keep the ball, no penalty stroke incurred.

Russell goes out to patrons' cars to help them if the customer is elderly. Now *that* is Southern hospitality.

One regular customer, now in her seventies, said this to a reporter from Myrtle Beach: "I can find things in here I cannot find in town. I buy castor oil, pliers for my pump, and a lot of things at Cooper's. It's cheaper here. I raised up all my kids here, and my eldest son is fifty. As a matter of fact, I am going to cook up this bacon in the morning for me and my children to eat with grits."

The only mistake that Cooper's has ever made is that they recently painted the store. But time will cure that.

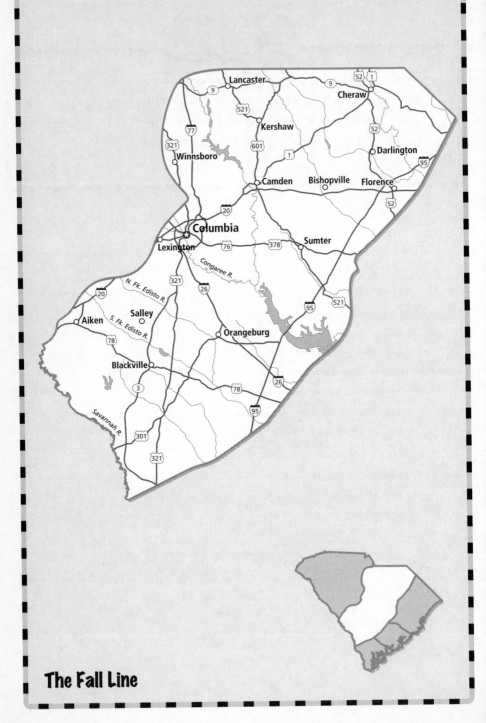

Lancaster

9

521

77

321

Winnsboro

Kershaw

601

1

9

52　1

Cheraw

52

Darlington

95

Camden

Bishopville

Florence

52

20

Columbia

Lexington

76

378

Sumter

Congaree R.

N. Fk. Edisto R.

321

26

20

Salley

S. Fk. Edisto R.

Aiken

78

Orangeburg

95

521

Blackville

3

78

26

Savannah R.

301

95

321

The Fall Line

4

The Fall Line

The Fall Line, sometimes called "the Midlands," is defined differently
by almost everyone who uses the term. But generally speaking it refers
to that geographical zone midway through the state of South Carolina.
It effectively separates what's known as the Upcountry from what they
call the Lowcountry. It has geographical earmarks all its own and a
population as diverse and eccentric as anywhere else. This area includes
South Carolina's capital city of Columbia, which has a colorful history, a
dramatic political heritage, and some of the most interesting personalities in the state.

Above the Fall Line the land is higher, fertile, rocky, and quick to
drain. Below that line the land is low, the soil is sandy, and the drain-
age system is widely diffused. The rainfall drains into a myriad of shallow rivers and creeks, and gently flowing swamps—all slow-moving
water. The Fall Line was where the ocean met the land when the world
was younger and the sea level was higher.

This land spawned interesting people like Dizzy Gillespie, jazz musician and hometown boy made good. Stack him up against Jody Pendarvis, who currently operates a welcome center for passing UFOs. This is
also the home of Emily Geiger, who singlehandedly beguiled her way
through enemy lines in the American Revolution with life-saving military
secrets. We have a ghost from the Fall Line; meet Agnes of Glasgow.
The annual Carolina Cup brings out everyone's competitive nature.
There's even gold in them thar hills. Go see what you can find.

Bar B Que's Battleground

One of the quickest ways to pick a fight in South Carolina is to claim to have the best recipe for pork Bar B Que. The difference (like in real estate) is *location, location, location.* Upcountry folks serve their Bar B Que with spicy tomato-based sauce. In the Midlands, no one would dream of making Bar B Que without a tangy mustard sauce. Down in the Lowcountry Bar B Que starts with a vinegar base that clears the sinuses and whets the appetite. Preferences are hard-wired from childhood on in Southerners, and arguing over favorites is a complete waste of time.

Roadside Bar B Que joints proliferate on backroads and byways of the Palmetto State.

★ ★

Horsing Around in Aiken
Aiken

Aiken is one of the prettiest towns in South Carolina. Like Augusta, Camden, and Pinehurst, it was on one of the early rail lines. Aiken got its name from the first president of the South Carolina Canal and Railroad Company, and with the popularity of rail travel after the 1840s, it began to attract wealthy Charlestonians who built elaborate summer homes there to escape the miasmas of the Lowcountry. After the Civil War it recovered quickly and became a winter destination for wealthy Northerners who began to establish what they called the "Winter

Aiken's glory days—past and present—as a player in the international world of horse racing are handsomely captured here.

★ ★

Colony" in Aiken. They also brought with them their affection for thoroughbred horses, and before long a training track was built, and a sporting industry was born. Today, Aiken's wide streets and gracious parkways recall those halcyon days, and it's still a social hub for the horsey set.

There's a museum in Aiken that recounts that era beautifully. The Aiken Thoroughbred Racing Hall of Fame and Museum is a horse of a different color as museums go. Exhibits celebrate the noble sport of horse racing and Aiken's important role in the American history of the sport from 1900 to the present. Thirty-nine champion thoroughbreds have trained at the prestigious Aiken Training Track, and each is remembered in the Hall of Fame. Exhibits here include photographs, trophies, racing silks, and other memorabilia from the careers of these flat racers and steeplechase horses. For example, the MacKenzie "Mack" Miller Exhibit features the trainer of the 1993 Kentucky Derby winner, Sea Hero.

The Museum is on the grounds of the former Hopelands estate, now a fourteen-acre public garden at 135 Dupree Street. It's open Tuesday through Sunday afternoons for most of the year, but only on weekends during the summer months of June through August. For more information, visit www.aikenracinghalloffame.com or call (803) 642-7650. It's an interesting place to visit—you can bet on it.

All Hail the Button King
Bishopville

It all started when bluegrass musician Dalton Stevens was having one of those sleepless nights. He tossed and turned and finally gave up and sewed a couple of buttons on his denim britches nearby. He found the exercise soothing, so he did some more—buttons that is. One button led to another and many, many sleepless nights later he had covered his entire pants with buttons, so he moved on to the jacket. A couple of years later the jacket too was covered in buttons—16,333 of them, and the suit now weighed sixteen pounds. His guitar came next and so

How many buttons does it take to create the Button King's world? He's shown here playing his guitar next to his "throne."
PHOTO BY HARROD BLANK, WWW.HARRODBLANK.COM. BUTTON HEARSE
AND ITEMS BELONG TO DALTON STEVENS, WWW.SCBUTTONKING.COM.

did 3,005 more buttons glued to the surface. It took 517 more to cover his shoes. By this time Mr. Stevens's button fetish was gaining some notoriety. He was approached by the local press, interviewed on the radio, and appeared on Florence's WPDE television station. This button thing was really working for him, and he started calling himself "The Button King." Of course there would be more buttons—lots more.

He used 226,000 buttons to cover his outhouse including the flush toilet inside. Of course he buttoned down his piano as part of his act.

It took 149,000 buttons to cover his Chevrolet Chevette and 600,000 to cover the hearse that one day will carry him to his grave. He bought and covered two caskets, one of which will eventually take him to the Big Button Sewing Box in the sky. In the meantime, Dalton Stevens continues to make music in his own inimitable way, and he has made it to the network talk shows, schmoozing with David Letterman and talking buttons with Johnny Carson; he even caught the attention of Charles Kuralt, who knew a thing or two about curiosities. He was also featured in a movie called *Automorphosis* by Harrod Blank in 2008. If you're in the neighborhood of Bishopville, why not stop by and pay homage to the Button King. He doesn't charge visitors for seeing his button collection, but he'll take donations to further sustain his growing museum of button art.

To find him go to 55 Joe Dority Road, visit www.scbuttonking.com, or call (803) 428-3841. For more on the film, see www.automorphosis.com.

South Carolina's Own Mr. Scissorhands
Bishopville

It's so bizarre—at first it sounds like a fable: a man whose whole life and philosophy revolve around a topiary garden. But then the photographic views of his garden are so enchanting the story must be true. Pearl Fryar had a knack with plants. It started in 1984 when a casual visit and the purchase of a $2 plant at a local nursery was embellished by a five-minute lesson on topiary pruning from the nurseryman. He went home and started trimming the shrubbery around his front door, shaping it, and encouraging its growth according to his artistic sensibilities. From that modest beginning sprang a hobby that became a career and a way of life.

When the front door topiary was done, Pearl filled his surrounding yard with other designs. His collection continued to grow while neighbors marveled at his talent and creativity. Many of his garden's newest trees and shrubs were salvaged from the discard piles of area growers and resurrected into living sculpture.

Snip, snip, hooray!

Eventually, his entire three-acre property on the outskirts of Bish-opville, South Carolina, became a fantasy land of twisted shapes and whimsical contours that sprang from Mr. Fryar's unbridled font of new ideas celebrating light, shadow, texture, height, balance, and symmetry. He called it his expression of peace, love, and goodwill. His efforts have been heralded around the world in magazine articles, television pro-grams, interviews, and talk shows. His garden has been designated a Preservation Project of the Garden Conservancy, who advocate for sav-ing and presenting America's exceptional gardens for educational pur-poses. Best of all, you can see it for yourself; the garden is presented to

★ ★

the public for free. Donations are welcome and used for the care and maintenance of the site. Don't be surprised if you encounter Mr. Fryar himself. He tends to his pruning as he tends the visitors flocking to his garden with his ample supply of love, patience, humor, and refreshing humility.

Visit www.pearlfryartopiary.com for hours and directions.

Taste of Heaven
Blackville

There's a natural artesian spring near Blackville in Barnwell County that belongs to God Almighty. It was deeded to Him on July 21, 1944, in the settlement of the estate of Mr. L. C. Boylston, so apparently it belongs to Him free and clear, but this was not an act of generosity.

Where believers drink to good health

Mr. Boylston was simply returning the property to its rightful owner.

From this wellspring had come miracle healings, according to the Native Americans living on these lands long before white men arrived. It first came to the attention of soldiers during the Revolutionary War when its healing waters cured four seriously wounded English loyalists serving under British general Banastre Tarleton. According to the legend after several weeks of drinking these curative waters, the men were fit to return to battle. After this the spring's fame for its astonishing healing powers had spread far and wide.

The still-flowing spring attracts enthusiastic believers even today. Cars, trucks, and trailers of all stripes stop by and fill up jugs of this water on a daily basis. The best part is—it's free. The Lord charges nothing for the water other than good behavior and a loving heart. If you're feeling poorly and are so inclined, you can stop by and taste these heavenly waters for yourself. Drive three miles north of Blackville on Highway 3, turn right on Healing Springs Road, then right (south) on SC S-6-538. The spring is about 150 yards south of the Healing Springs Baptist Church.

A Table Set by Faith

Blackville

To be honest, telling someone to go out of their way and go to Blackville to eat is really a bit of a stretch. There are lifelong residents of South Carolina who do not know how to get to Blackville. This small community of nearly three thousand souls is not on any tourist's must-do list except for Miller's Bread Basket, a restaurant owned, staffed, and operated by a Mennonite family serving Pennsylvania Dutch food with a Southern touch.

We're talking about meat loaf, fried chicken, and fresh-from-the-garden vegetables, yeast rolls, macaroni and cheese, and mashed potatoes with pan gravy in copious amounts. Your meal is finished off with a choice of homemade pies like coconut cream, German chocolate, and lemon meringue. There's even shoofly pie—if your heart can

★ ★

**Quality ingredients, traditional skills,
hospitality, and faith—this recipe
is in daily use here.**

take it. The decor is simple and free of pretension; it offers comfort
and warmth instead. The service is genuinely offered without unneces-
sary flair.

Customers come from all over the state, but they are only customers once. After that first visit, a customer becomes a friend. Owners
Ray and his wife, Susie, are just plain good folks to the core. They do
two things extremely well. They give very good value for the dollar in

their restaurant. They also run a bakery and gift shop next door where the cinnamon raisin loaf alone is enough to keep you coming back, time and again. Permeating the entire enterprise is the home-sweet-home aroma of freshly baked bread.

So the next time someone tells you that you have lost your mind to go to Blackville to eat lunch, remind them about the cinnamon raisin bread. Then give them these directions. Miller's Bread Basket is in Barnwell County on US 78 at 483 Main Street. Call (803) 284-3117 or visit www.millersbread-basket.com.

Blenheim—the Ginger Ale That Packs a Punch
Blenheim

The recipe dates from 1903. Take water from a natural artesian spring in South Carolina's Marlboro County (Pee Dee region) and combine it with strong, spicy Jamaican ginger. The result is a concoction known as Blenheim Ginger Ale—the taste of which one is unlikely to ever forget. The formula for this unlikely concoction stemmed from the mind of Dr. C. R. May, who in the late 1800s was looking for a way to disguise the distaste of plain mineral water as a cure for dyspepsia. Its medicinal usefulness turned out to be disappointing, but the spicy taste had legs of its own and attracted a modest following.

The original company bubbled along for eight decades with only regional awareness from the public. In 1983 a bottle of Blenheim Ginger Ale found its way into a feature on the nationally broadcast television program *PM Magazine,* and the secret was out. By 1985 this racy soft drink was mentioned in *Playboy* magazine, of all places, which added considerably to its reputation. When Charles Kuralt described it on his folksy travelogue for CBS, called *On the Road,* the ingredients of a national demand were added to the recipe. In 1993 entrepreneur extraordinaire Alan Schafer (founder of South of the Border; see "You Never Sausage a Place," page 111) saw the mass market potential for this unique product. He bought the company, and moved its manufacturing operation to a larger plant within his tourist destination at

★ ★

South Carolina's best kept secret

Hamer, South Carolina. The original bottling plant in Blenheim became a working museum of the bottlers' art.

Still, Blenheim Ginger Ale is somewhat hard to find. You can order it online at www.blenheimshrine.com, or, if you're lucky, you can find it in a few specialty outlets in the Carolinas. As the Blenheim cult followers are quick to tell you, it is an acquired taste. The *New York Times* summed it up this way: "The first swallow brings on a four-sneeze fit. The second one clears out the sinuses and leaves the tongue and throat throbbing with prickly heat."

Bless Their Hearts— All of Them

We were raised by our mamas to always be polite. There is not a mother in South Carolina who has not admonished her children, "If you can't say something nice about another person, then don't say anything at all." And so, we took it to heart. That became part of the rules of life, right along with, "don't chew with your mouth open, and don't eat with your elbows on the table."

But there were times when one simply had to comment on a fellow Southerner's behavior. True blue South Carolinians know that when a sentence begins with someone else's name followed by "bless her heart," you are bound to hear some semi-true trash.

"Did you see that outfit Sara Jane had on? Bless her heart, she tries, but. . . ." "John Henry Jones, bless his heart, should know that stripes and plaids don't match. . . ."

Now you know. You can trash someone perfectly, if you just say, "bless her/his heart."

"Welcome to Planet Earth!"

Bowman

Jody Pendarvis believes in being prepared. His life's ambition, it appears, is to be ready and welcoming when the aliens from outer space come down to Earth. He has gone so far as to build his own UFO Welcome Center on his property in Bowman, South Carolina, dedicated to that goal. To say he is eccentric may be an

How do you say "y'all come see me, ya hear" in alien-ese?

understatement, but he's seriously anticipating a visit from outer space any day. He reads about it, thinks about it, and talks about it endlessly. He constantly embellishes his intergalactic welcome center to make it more comfortable for his anticipated guests.

Construction began on his project in 1994 without blueprint or plan. It eventually took the shape of a flying saucer from a 1950s sci-fi film long forgotten. The propulsion of this vehicle is quite mysterious, but Jody insists it is capable of flight. It stands forty-six feet wide—the same diameter as most UFOs according to Jody, who watches these things closely. Later he added a second smaller saucer on top of his

★ ★

homemade spaceship, so the aliens could take him with them to outer space. Be prepared for the spaceship to be a work in progress. Scraps of metal and superfluous electronic gear are strewn about the place. Excess building materials and other discards from Jody's earthly life are scattered throughout the grounds indicating that, apparently, aliens aren't sticklers when it comes to housekeeping.

So far his guest book lists no interplanetary visitors; however people from here on Earth stop by with some regularity. For a few bucks Jody Pendarvis will greet you and offer a tour of his UFO Welcome Center. He doesn't seem to be dismayed that no aliens have shown up so far. He just wants to be ready when they come, with open arms and a great big South Carolina "hello."

The telephone book has a listing for the UFO Welcome Center, which is (803) 829-2311. Deciding exactly how to list Jody in the phone directory proved to be a bit of a challenge. After some deliberations a category was created under the listing, "Space Research and Development." But we don't recommend calling ahead for reservations. Jody seldom answers his phone. He's far too busy monitoring the skies. It's a better bet to look for his spotted pickup truck and knock gently on the door of his trailer. The UFO Welcome Center is located at 4004 Homestead Road in Bowman. Take I-95 to exit 82. Travel west for nine miles toward Bowman, turning right on Homestead Road. Jody's saucer will be visible on the left.

Merry Mayhem in Boykin
Boykin

Holiday parades are not unusual phenomena in most American cities and towns. They are usually held some time between Thanksgiving and New Year's to officially usher in the holiday season of gift giving, carol singing, and grab-your-wallet merchandising. Two famous examples are Macy's Thanksgiving Day Parade in New York and the Tournament of Roses Parade in Pasadena, California. But no tour of holiday parades is complete without a visit to the Boykin Christmas

★ ★

People-watching is the main sport at the Boykin Christmas Parade.
COURTESY OF THE BOYKIN CHRISTMAS PARADE COMMITTEE

Parade held in the town of Boykin (population 200), nestled in the midlands of South Carolina. They take the concept to a completely 'nother realm.

On the Sunday before Christmas, the festivities get underway. Every year the parade changes and entries, vendors, and sponsors come and go as the mood strikes. Some of the recent events have included the Road Kill BBQ Cook-off and gospel concert choirs singing at Swift Creek Baptist Church. Pickup trucks and farm wagons make the transformation into floats for the occasion, several of which have made repeat appearances over the years. Favorites have included The Red Neck Yacht Club, and the Root Beer Float. The appreciative crowd includes nearly every dog in the county dressed to the nines in holiday garb; the canines howl their approval and may spontaneously weave in and out of the parade. Holding court over the entire scene is the Fat Back Queen, usually a burly farmer dressed in drag who waves graciously at the adoring spectators from the throne atop her gaily decorated float.

Of course no Christmas parade is complete without the arrival of jolly ole St. Nick. Only in Boykin he arrives in a conveyance a little more quirky than a sleigh and nine flying reindeer. Once he came in on an airplane; another time he rode a horse. Several times he made his entrance on a farm tractor, and once Mr. and Mrs. Claus arrived seated on a gold satin sofa held high in the air by a forklift. You just never know.

It's not that the people of Boykin have no respect for the holidays; it's just that their enthusiasm gets the better of them. So energetic were they over the past few years that the whole thing was called off on account of liability issues as the crowd swelled into the thousands. This respite from the parade was equally unacceptable, so it's all back and, thankfully, so is the fun. The festivities usually begin around 2 p.m., but get there early and bring your own lawn chair. From I-20 take exit 98 (US 521, Sumter, Camden) and bear right. Continue onto SC 261 East and look for the crowd on Main Street. See www.the boykinparade.com for more.

Choo Choo, Puff Puff, Ding Dong
Branchville

Although the first railroad in the world began in Charleston in 1830 and ran 136 miles to Hamburg in Aiken County (see "The Hiss-tory of the *Best Friend*," page 189), the town of Branchville has a claim to fame as well. The rousing success of the original rail line fostered another line built from Branchville, one of the stops along the way,

reaching across the Midlands to Columbia, the state's fast-growing
capital. This meant that Branchville was the location of the first railroad junction in 1838. Today, that fact is remembered and celebrated
in a quaint but fascinating railroad museum in the old depot. It's also
the inspiration for a local intentionally misspelled event called Raylrode
Daze Festivul every September. Call the Branchville Town Hall to schedule a tour at (803) 274-8820 or visit www.raylrodedazefestivul.com for
more details.

The old depot makes an appropriate stop for a review of
early South Carolina railroading.

Tales of the Underground
Camden

The South Carolina towns of Camden near Columbia, Ninety Six near Greenwood, and Cowpens near Spartanburg are popular with Revolutionary War re-enactors. It seems you can hardly throw a rock in these towns without hitting a famous battleground or historic graveyard.

The Old Quaker Graveyard in Camden is a case in point. This is the final resting place of Abraham Lincoln's brother-in-law, who was a Confederate doctor, a notorious female spy for the Confederacy, and several Civil War generals. It also holds the grave of a celebrated

Here lies the sad story of Agnes of Glasgow.

Confederate soldier named Richard Kirkland who mercifully gave water to dying Union soldiers on the battlefield at Fredericksburg. Visitors to the churchyard still find token water bottles and canteens on his grave left in homage to his valor.

But best known of all is the haunted grave of Agnes of Glasgow. Back in America's colonial days she was a beautiful young lassie in Scotland madly in love with her soldier beau. His name was Lt. Angus McPherson, and he was destined to go overseas with British troops attempting to quell the burgeoning revolution there. So deep was Agnes's anguish over the separation from her fiancé that she stowed away on an American-bound ship and crossed the Atlantic to follow him. Her ship landed in Charleston, where she was told her lover was stationed upcountry near Camden.

Unfortunately, when she got there no trace of her soldier could be found. To add to her dismay, she had become quite ill, and sometime in 1780 she died and was buried in the Quaker churchyard where they say she still wanders aimlessly through the headstones looking for the lost love she never saw again.

To find the Old Quaker Graveyard take I-20 to exit 98. Travel 1.4 miles toward Camden on US 521, then turn left on Meeting Street. Agnes of Glasgow's gravesite is before the gated entrance to the graveyard. It is inside a small brick wall off to the left behind the Revolutionary War Park and Old Presbyterian Cemetery. (If you pass Church Street on the right you have gone too far.)

Our Cup Runneth Over
Camden

This is South Carolina's answer to the Kentucky Derby. It's called the Carolina Cup, and it's a horse race with a familiar song of life in South Carolina. Someone once said of it, "I went for eight straight years and never saw a horse. . . ."

Camden, South Carolina, is famous for two things. First, it was home to multiple armed conflicts in the American Revolution. A recent movie called *The Patriot* starring Mel Gibson had its roots in Camden. Secondly, in the last fifty years or so, it has been host to a giant cocktail party that also includes a steeplechase. Can anyone imagine a cocktail party attended by over fifty thousand folk?

In the last couple of decades, "The Cup," as it is now known, has signaled the first day of spring, and the start of the party season for anyone old enough to drink. There are thousands of ladies in hats dressed in the latest Lilly Pulitzer, and gentlemen in either madras or seersucker and Weejuns, who gently guide themselves to various parking spaces that are now so rare they're being passed down to the next generation. Tickets to The Cup are as valuable as tickets to The Masters.

Oh, for sure, the horse races actually do take place, and there are numerous betting spots, but in truth, most folks don't really care. The college crowd tends to morph toward spots where copious amounts of "PJ" (Purple Juice) are consumed. PJ recipes are passed down through the college years, and the recipes do vary slightly, depending on which fraternity is mixing. But most varieties seem to contain large amounts of grain alcohol (200 proof and tasteless), thoroughly disguised with grape juice and at least one can of Donald Duck Orange Juice. Almost every year, someone shows up with a goosefoot bathtub full of PJ in the back of a station wagon. Of course, it does not taste like liquor, and that is the point.

For decades The Cup was bankrolled by Mrs. Marion duPont Scott until it finally became self-supporting. Mrs. Scott was a genuine duPont who married a movie star of her era named Randolph Scott, all of which defined her as a blueblood by birth and deed. Mrs. Scott was still attending The Cup well into her nineties. Up until she died some years back, the tradition was to start the Carolina Cup by having brunch with Mrs. Scott at The Pinetree Hunt Club.

In 1963 a sudden prolonged downpour occurred just as the party was gathering steam. The only problem occurred when the rain caused those souls wearing madras to look like gooey rainbows, and ladies

removed their Papagallos, and strolled barefoot to the next space. The
following Sunday, *The State* newspaper printed a photo of an enthusiastic racing fan holding an umbrella with only the ribs left intact.

Next spring, we'll see you at The Cup. Visit www.carolinacup.com
for more.

What Ever Happened to Granby?
Cayce

When you set your GPS to take you to Granby, South Carolina, don't
get too upset if it blows a gasket, throws sparks, and falls off the
windshield. No such place exists. Not anymore. A place called Granby
did exist, however, and it has an interesting story.

It all began with an Indian village on the banks of Congaree Creek.
After colonial traders began doing business here with greater frequency, it soon became evident that a trading post should be built. An
agreement with the local Cherokee Indians in 1716 made this possible.
By 1748 the trading post was joined by a fort. James Chesnut and
Joseph Kershaw built an early general store next to the fort in 1765.
It must have dazzled settlers, who were surprised to see a two-story
building in such an unsettled place. It must have been built well, too,
because it lasted nearly two hundred years. Thereafter people began
to arrive more steadily, and they started to call the place "Granby."
During the Revolutionary War, when it was called "Fort Granby," it
was the site of several skirmishes between our boys and the Brits.
After the war South Carolina grew like a weed, and Granby grew with
it. In fact it became the capital of Lexington County in 1785. That may
be why Granby was worthy of a visit from President George Washington on his 1791 Southern Tour of the brand new nation.

In 1802 Granby had twice as many houses as Columbia, across the
river. All seemed well for this growing metropolis, but Mother Nature
had another plan. Frequent flooding by the Congaree was a constant
threat, and soon the government seat moved to the nearby town
of Lexington, because it was built on higher ground. Apparently the

Granby's Trading Post recalls the town that is no more.

inhabitants chose a similar path. So when America's first architect general, Robert Mills, happened to visit the site in 1826, he observed that "nobody was there."

To learn more about the vanished town of Granby, visit the Cayce Historical Museum at the City of Cayce Municipal Complex, 1800 12th Street, Cayce. Call (803) 739-5385 or visit www.cityofcayce-sc.gov for more.

★ ★

Bebopping with "The Diz"
Cheraw

Anyone who knows and loves the uniquely American idiom of jazz knows the name Dizzy Gillespie. His oddly bent trumpet and blowfish cheeks were his trademarks. He was instrumental in the development of modern jazz and bebop in the 1930s, '40s, and '50s, played with most of the big bands of the Swing Era, popularized Afro-Cuban jazz, and is credited with being the inspiration to many jazz greats including Miles Davis.

Far lesser known is the fact that "The Diz" was a South Carolina boy and was born and raised in the small town of Cheraw in the state's Pee Dee region. The year was 1917, and at birth he was given the name John Birks Gillespie. He was the youngest of nine children. After his father's death when the boy was only ten, life was hard for the family, but he remembered it later as being a time when "mischief, money making and music captured all my attention." He played the piano and the trombone in local gigs around Cheraw. His natural sense of rhythm and unique flair for melody were eventually his ticket to stardom.

He died in New Jersey in 1993, but his sound, style, and musicality are available to future generations through recordings, films, and videotaped performances—all of which continue to build his fame. Although he belongs to the world, the keeper of his flame seems to be Cheraw. Each year a jazz festival is held in his honor, and young jazz artists from all over the world make a pilgrimage to his South Carolina home. A tall bronze statue of The Diz stands in Cheraw's Town Green. It captures the essence of the man with his akimbo trumpet and signature cheeks with affectionate warmth and reality. It is a focal point of the town's pride in Dizzy Gillespie, the man and his music. Check out www.cheraw.com and www.scjazzfestival.com for more.

**The memorial statue to "The Diz"
captures him on a high note.**
SOUTH CAROLINA JAZZ FESTIVAL, CHERAW, SC

★ ★

A Bite of the Big Apple
Columbia

Culture wonks and sociologists tend to disagree on this, but the nick-
name for New York City (for a long time now) has been "The Big
Apple," and the Big Apple dance of the 1930s—which originated in
South Carolina—is one of the contenders for the reason why.

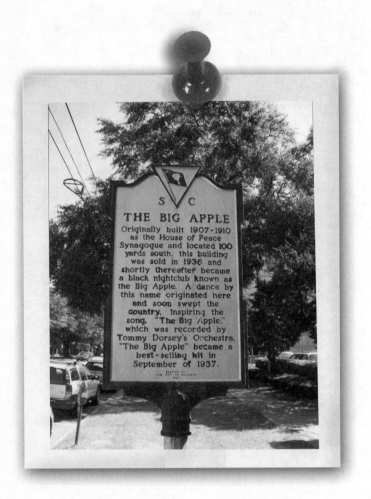

An inauspicious birthplace for such an energetic jive

★ ★

Here's what we know for sure; the earliest known gestures and body movements vaguely resembling the dance known as the Big Apple were seen on Southern plantations danced by enslaved African Americans during religious ceremonies. The movements are part of a group dance called the "ring shout," and these basic steps evolved through the years into a social expression. In the 1930s a nightclub housed in a former synagogue on Columbia's Park Street became the place to go to dance the ring shout. So popular was this nightspot with its jive music and busy dance floor that white students from the University of South Carolina started coming by to watch. The nightclub was called The Big Apple, and so the dance being done there so joyfully came to be called The Big Apple too.

It was only a matter of time until the Big Apple made its debut on the dance floor at the Myrtle Beach Pavilion. From there it traveled to New York, where it caught the attention of a talent agent, Gay Foster, who was booking talent for an upcoming show at the Roxy Theater, second largest theater in the world at the time. She hired eight couples from South Carolina who did the Big Apple six shows a day for three whole weeks before sold-out crowds. In no time at all the Big Apple was seen in trendy night clubs and ballrooms throughout New York City. From there it was a short hop to Hollywood where the Big Apple was featured in several musicals of the late 1930s. Even comedian Bob Hope made a joke about the Big Apple in one of his popular comedies. Arthur Murray added the Big Apple to his repertoire of must-learn social dances and sent it out to the rest of the country through his franchise dance studios. The Tommy Dorsey Orchestra recorded a song called "The Big Apple" which became a hit on the radio in 1937.

Fads come and go and so do dance crazes. The Big Apple has long since vanished from the dance floors of America but "The Big Apple" as a nickname for New York City lingers, which is strong testimony to the power and viability of popular culture—not a bad gig for a little dance from South Carolina.

Where the Forecast Is Always Blue Skies
Columbia

Tradition says great art should transport the viewer to a higher beauty
or a stark reality. But on the other hand, famous South Carolina artist Blue Sky leads thousands of his viewers smack dab into the side
of a building—right up against a brick wall. Drivers along Columbia's
Taylor Street (between Marion and Bull Streets) suddenly encounter an
unexpected detour. Looming before them through their windshield is a
huge mural. It depicts a roadway tunneling through mountain rock to
a distant sunset in the far beyond.

Optimistic "Tunnelvision" always portrays
light at the end of the tunnel.

What canine
dreams are
made of?

The work called "Tunnelvision" is painted on the side of the AgFirst Farm Credit Bank building in downtown Columbia. The artist who calls himself "Blue Sky" was born Warren Edward Johnson in South Carolina's capital city in 1938. He was already a figure in South Carolina's art world, but not yet well known as a muralist when he began this project in 1974.

The artist recounted that his inspiration was labored: "I'd already seen the wall, I'd sat and studied it for hours, just waiting to see what would come before my eyes . . . nothing came. [Then] early one morning, I woke up [from a dream] and it was there . . . [immediately] I sketched it. . . .That's why I call it 'Tunnelvision,' because it was a vision in a dream."

"Tunnelvision" is a happy marriage between technical ability and insightful vision. Blue Sky has a special knack for taking the viewer on a journey to something familiar but depicted in a refreshing new light. "Tunnelvision" isn't alone in Blue Sky's amazing body of work. He's equally adept in the world of sculpture. Nearby on Taylor Street is "Busted Plug Plaza," a battered fire hydrant made of metal, towering four stories high and weighing 675,000 pounds. A couple of blocks away is "Neverbust," a massive chain linking two separate buildings on Main Street.

Blue Sky's quirky art is always unexpected and never dull. His unique realism has fooled many a viewer and startled drivers, pedestrians, and even a dog or two trying to lift his leg over an outsized target. See more at www.blueskyart.com.

Mystery on the State House Grounds
Columbia

South Carolina's State House as it stands today was under construction in the heart of downtown Columbia when the Civil War began. Every child in the state learns the story of how the unfinished walls of the State House sustained Union artillery and rifle fire. (See "Shooting Stars over South Carolina," page 188.) They hear how the building

Here lies Captain Lunsford, who has a curious hold on some State House real estate.

was left unfinished until the war was well over, and the official dedication didn't occur until 1903. This makes the State House and the grounds unusual by definition, but few people know that there is a lone grave in the southwest corner of the State House grounds surrounded by a wrought iron fence almost hidden by a stand of trees. This is the grave of Captain Swanson Lunsford, who was born in Virginia and died in 1799 at the age of forty years. It is unclear why this early grave would be preserved intact, especially for a man who wasn't even born in South Carolina. Indeed, it's unusual that a state house would include any graves among its outdoor statues and commemorative monuments.

★ ★

It is known that Lunsford was a Revolutionary War officer who served under "Lighthorse Harry" Lee during the Carolina Campaign of 1780, and his exploits were by all accounts exemplary and heroic. Some sources say that Lunsford owned some of the land on which the State House was eventually built. And that may be why his grave was left undisturbed. Others say South Carolinians all love a hero, and his wartime service alone may account for his burial site in a highly public place. Nevertheless his eighteenth-century gravestone, now almost illegible, is still there. Today, it is surrounded by a modern marker set in place by Lunsford's descendants in 1953.

The oddity of Captain Lunsford's grave being preserved at its original site when the State House was first planned is one thing. The fact that it stayed there through wartime, and the equally corrosive effects of a bustling metropolis growing up around it, is quite another. Only Captain Lunsford knows why, and he's not saying a word.

The Battle of the Palmetto State
Columbia

The football rivalry that exists between the Clemson University Tigers and the University of South Carolina Gamecocks is the longest uninterrupted series in the South. It all began back in 1896 when Clemson coach Walter Riggs scheduled a competitive matchup with rival South Carolina College for a Thursday in October coinciding with Columbia's festive State Fair. (See "Meet Yo' Mama at the Rocket," page 183.) The rivalry came to a head early on with the 1902 game (which Carolina won 12–6). This is when the Gamecock first appeared as Carolina's official mascot. (See "Just So You'll Know," page 200.) The crowd's enthusiasm reached such a fevered pitch that a near riot broke out after the game. Dozens of fans required medical attention, and for safety reasons the annual game between these rivals was cancelled until 1909.

The emotional energy did not diminish with the passage of time. In 1946 counterfeit tickets were sold displacing from the stadium legitimate ticket holders who were unfairly barred from attending. Disgruntled fans stormed the gates and were eventually allowed in to watch the game standing along the sidelines. Things got out of hand when a Clemson fan supposedly strangled a live chicken at midfield during halftime. The bedlam that ensued required intervention by South Carolina's political guru U.S. Secretary of State James F. Byrnes, and the venerable Strom Thurmond, soon to be governor. Only then was order restored to the passionate crowd. Hardly anyone noticed Carolina took the day, 26–14.

By the 1950s Big Thursday had become a Southern institution. Men came to the game in suits and ties, and wives and coeds dressed in the latest fall fashions. Parades, parties, and tailgate celebrations amplified by the hoopla of the State Fair all swelled to elaborate proportions and for a very long time it was nothing but fun. Even the *New York Times* got in the act with feature stories covering this famous athletic and social event in South Carolina's calendar year.

Just when fans thought they'd seen it all, a prank in 1961 stole the show. A Carolina fraternity donned uniforms similar to the Clemson Tigers' and rushed onto the field before anyone else for pregame warmups, confusing the crowd. Even the Clemson band was fooled and began to play their fight song, "Tiger Rag." The imposters' comic antics on the field mocked the real team's prowess by fumbling catches and tripping over their own feet. Angry Clemson fans, unhappy at being fooled, stormed onto the field, and a melee ensued.

By the 1960s the Big Thursday game was rescheduled to a more conventional Saturday date, but the fervor of the rivalry still goes on. In fact it was recently the subject of a continuing education class at USC called "Back to Big Thursday" indoctrinating a new generation into the slings and arrows of this most colorful and sometimes outrageous Palmetto tradition.

A Dream Built to Scale

Columbia

L. C. Carson was a builder in Orangeburg, South Carolina. He loved his work, did a fine job, and over the course of a lifetime career, he built hundreds of homes and commercial buildings and made a significant contribution to his hometown. But he always harbored a secret dream—to lend his skill to the creation of some of the world's great architecture. In short he wanted to be a part of architectural history itself.

The desire and ambition stayed with him for years, and as he neared retirement it became apparent to him that this dream might never be fulfilled. One day he started working with some surplus materials from one of his construction sites, and he started to fashion a miniature building that began to look like one of his fantasies. He found the work satisfying. That miniature led to another and another until he had built a miniature city of temples, churches, public monuments, and architectural wonders from all over the world. The structures eventually numbered thirty-five in total. These waist-high replicas were described by locals as the "Concrete City." In time the collection developed an identity and a kind of fame all its own. Soon people from all over the state were coming to see Mr. Carson's backyard village of the Roman Coliseum, the Cathedral of Notre Dame, the Great Pyramids of Giza, the Sphinx, even the Hanging Gardens of Babylon.

In the twilight of his life he realized he had accomplished his dream after all. He had participated in the building of some of the great architectural monuments of all time—only built to his scale and timetable. Shortly before his death in 1998 he donated the Concrete City to the South Carolina State Museum in Columbia where many of his small buildings can be seen today. That was the fulfillment of another dream—that his work would be preserved and exhibited after he was gone. For more information visit www.southcarolinastatemuseum.org.

Downsized icons of architecture on display under one roof
IMAGE FROM ORIGINAL COURTESY OF THE SOUTH CAROLINA
STATE MUSEUM, COLUMBIA, SC

Show Me the Money

Columbia

What ever happened to Confederate money? We know where it was printed and what happened to the printing plant per se, but the history of Confederate currency continues to unfold today.

When the Secession Convention met in Charleston in December 1860, the printing company known as Evans & Cogswell was engaged to print the minutes of the meetings and soon became principal printer

Folks shop here for groceries these days, but we regret to inform you Confederate money is not accepted.

for the Confederacy. Their duties eventually included the printing of the official Ordinance of Secession, the soldier's prayer book, books on war tactics and medical practices, plus bonds and small denomination currency for the new government. The actual printing plant couldn't have been more conspicuous in its location on Broad Street in downtown Charleston. In fact that location proved to be problematic as the proximity to Charleston Harbor made it an easy target for Union naval artillery. It was decided to move this key function of the Confederate government to a safer location. The entire printing operation made the journey to Columbia and settled into a new building at the corner of Gervais and Huger Streets. It functioned there until the burning of Columbia by Union forces in February 1865. Naturally, the printing plant for Confederate currency was of special interest to General Sherman and his raiders. In the chaos of the fire, vast amounts of Confederate currency in various stages of printing were last seen being carried off by looting troops as souvenirs. General Sherman noted this specifically in his memoirs written after the war. Most of the printing equipment including the actual printing plates for Confederate money was destroyed.

When the fire was out and the smoke cleared, all that remained of Evans & Cogswell was a brick shell that eventually was rebuilt—like Columbia itself. First a new roof, then interior restoration gave the building new life. During the Temperance years, following the war, the state used it for warehousing liquor. This continued until 1907 when the distribution system collapsed, and the building was abandoned. During the 1930s as the Depression settled over the state's already devastated agricultural economy, the facility was used to dispense seeds through the U.S. Seed Loan Program. The next few decades saw tenants come and go from the deteriorating old printing plant. It warehoused paper and even furniture at different times. By the 1970s the building was derelict and in danger of being razed. But the city of Columbia recognized its historic value and its potential for redevelopment. In 1979 the old Confederate Printing Plant was listed on the National Register of Historic Places. A cooperative effort on behalf of the city and the Publix grocery store chain led to a landmark adaptive reuse in 2002. Now shoppers come and go exchanging money for food and other items in this historic setting, bringing the building into something of a financial full circle. Part of the structure itself was converted into chic condominiums, which sell for prices in the half million dollar range. So, who says Confederate money is worthless? Who has the last laugh now?

What Did George Washington Have to Do with It?
Columbia

The South Carolina State House was the scene of high drama and chaos when Union troops burned the city of Columbia on February 17, 1865, during the War Between the States. Even today, visitors to the seat of our state's government are shown the remaining scars on the outside walls of the building left by the strikes of Union artillery. The obvious pockmarks still in evidence are proudly displayed and designated by bronze stars. (See "Shooting Stars over South Carolina," page 188.)

Not so obvious is the elegant statue of President George Washington that faces Gervais Street and looks down Main where the fire once left a vast wasteland. Supposedly this life-size statue was the only one for which Washington himself posed during his lifetime. Only six castings were made of the original marble sculpture, and this one was sent to South Carolina where he was feted as an honored guest many times.

Poor George. He got his share of the drunken mob's attention on that fateful night in 1865. Along with the bricks and insults thrown at the bronze image of the president, something hit and broke off the president's slender cane. He appears to lean confidently on a walking stick that ends mysteriously somewhere near his shin.

How strange it is that the State House (under construction at the time) was completed after the war and is still in use today, but the statue of George Washington was never repaired. The piece of the cane was thought to have disappeared in the rubble and confusion of the fire. Amazingly the broken piece turned up and is on display today

What's wrong with this picture?

at the South Carolina Confederate Relic Room and Military Museum just a few blocks away from the State House grounds. His broken cane, like the artillery damage on the walls, was left for future generations to witness as proof of "Yankee evil." Here in South Carolina some insults are simply unforgivable. Visit www.crr.sc.gov for more.

★ ★

Needs More Salt
Columbia

The dizzy, wild enthusiasm of the Jazz Age found a welcome home in South Carolina when it was found that elements of iodine were higher in products from our state than from elsewhere. This trace element found in rocks, soils, plants, and animals is also found in the thyroid gland in human beings. Without the right balance of iodine, people get sick and develop an ugly swelling in their neck and jaw called a goiter.

It wasn't long before the benefits of South Carolina's iodine got touted in every conceivable advertising medium and public place. When the bandwagon took off, everybody wanted on. Radio station

**Before it read "The Palmetto State,"
it was all about iodine.**
IMAGE FROM ORIGINAL COURTESY OF THE SOUTH CAROLINA
STATE MUSEUM, COLUMBIA, SC

WIS, which was heard throughout the Midlands, had a nightly sign-off to the good people of the "Wonderful Iodine State." Our iodine-laden milk was deemed especially good for the development of children. It was said to prevent enlarged thyroids, and mental and physical birth defects. The same was true of our fruits and vegetables. We had a competitive edge for our homegrown produce over the Midwest and West Coast because of iodine, iodine, iodine. The iodine campaign reached its zenith when moonshine producers working in Hell Hole Swamp bragged about the benefits of iodine in their hooch, "Not a Goiter in a Gallon."

The campaign also found its way onto South Carolina automobile license plates in 1930. Under each number every plate read, "The Iodine State." When that got old, they changed it to "The Iodine Products State." (There's a collector's item for you.) The iodine craze continued for several years, but, alas, it petered out when it was learned that the net effort for South Carolina's agricultural products was unimpressive. In the 1940s iodized salt came on the market and was as handy as the corner grocery. The party was over for South Carolina's iodine campaign. It was a great run, and it sure seemed like a good idea at the time.

Meet Yo' Mama at the Rocket
Columbia

In mid-October, one of the mid-state's "must sees" is the State Fair. The dynamic that makes this seemingly ordinary fair entertaining is that it's truly a family affair—did we mention that it is a huge event? Tens of thousands of folk throughout the state spend at least one day at the fair. It is clean and well run. The fair is beautifully laid out, landscaped, and perfectly safe.

There are lots of fun events. Every day of the fair, there is a name, headline attraction at The Grandstand like Darius Rucker, formerly of Hootie and the Blowfish, a big-time rock band with local roots. Numerous barns are filled with livestock, birds of all kinds, and some zoo

★ ★

This empty rocket shell, a remnant of the
Cold War, is now the gateway to all that is
merry and fun. Hi-ho, come to the fair.

animals. Other contests are de rigueur including cake baking, quilts,
photography, art, and sideshows where you can win a teddy bear if
the carnies fail to guess your weight.

For many years, there was an iconic voice that ruled the public
address system. She was a true South Carolinian in that she tended to
mumble her words, and she used an everyday true Southern pronun-
ciation. Part of this story is the rocket. Sometime in the forgotten past,
some strings were pulled and a genuine NASA Titan rocket shell was

donated, and it guards the fair's main entrance. The rocket is huge, and it's visible from any place on the fairgrounds. One thing that you could count on was this lady's voice saying over and over, "Jimmy Jones, meet yo' mama at the rocket." The rocket is the favorite meeting place even today.

The State Fair is held at the State Fairgrounds at 1200 Rosewood Drive in Columbia. Come October, call (843) 799-3387 or (888) 444-3247, or visit www.scstatefair.org for details on times, exhibits, scheduled events, and admission prices.

Unweaving an Old Mystery
Columbia

When Olympia Mills opened for business in 1899, it was the most modern, technically advanced, and largest American cotton mill under one roof. It was the pride of Columbia, South Carolina. People came from all around the Midlands looking for jobs there. Sometimes whole families were employed by the mill including children, not an uncommon practice at the time. Raw cotton in huge bales arrived at the mill by train, where more than 1,200 looms processed it into thread and then cloth. Although the machinery moved very fast and had many exposed moving parts, Olympia was known as the most state-of-the-art textile operation of its day. Nobody seemed alarmed that the workforce included many young children who were employed in the extremely dangerous spinning room.

The story goes that mill supervisors told dawdling children who were not working up to capacity that they would be thrown into the furnace as punishment for missing their quotas. Today, such a practice seems unlikely, even for a time when lack of child labor laws spelled horror for untold numbers of children throughout the country.

They say "time doth all things repay." The textile industry has largely moved overseas, and the old Olympia Mills building is now an upscale apartment complex where residents live among the heavy timbers and textured walls in chic loft apartments. These days residents of Olympia

Luxury living or scene of the crime?

Mills are said to have something spooky to cope with as inhabitants of the historic building. Eerie sounds of children crying and tiny footsteps on the floors have been heard. People have noticed the mysterious disappearance or rearrangement of tools under lock and key. The toys belonging to the children of current residents are disturbed with some regularity, and the faces of small children and tiny handprints have been seen on the frosted windows on chilly winter mornings.

Are these the hauntings of children murdered by overzealous supervisors or is something else afoot? Did these children die at their posts and their bodies were burned to hide the evidence? What is known for sure is that child labor practices at Olympia Mills went unchanged for another four decades.

Born to Secede

It is a historical fact; South Carolina was the first state to secede from the Union during (what our great-grandmothers taught us to call) "the recent unpleasantness." But mostly unknown to those from the North, we are still exercising our penchant to secede.

Sometime around the early 1950s, Mr. Robert McClurkin Perry, president of the Bank of Kershaw, became increasingly perturbed. It appeared that the county line between Kershaw and Lancaster County ran right through the middle of his home. Although he had claimed Kershaw County as his home for years, paid taxes there, and voted there, Kershaw County became increasingly difficult to deal with, a problem mostly having to do with politics. Finally, Mr. Perry had had enough. He met in secret with the folks from Lancaster County. They told him they couldn't help him because, as a matter of law, precedence dictated that he was stuck in Kershaw County. Mr. Perry then met with the only lawyer in Kershaw, "Mush" Jones, to see what could be done. Mr. Jones said the simplest way to get relief was to secede from Kershaw County and join Lancaster County. Mr. Perry went at this idea with a quiet fury. He enlisted the aid of some of Kershaw's most notorious characters to circulate a petition for secession. These gentlemen decided it was in their best interest to aid Mr. Perry since, collectively—and here's the bottom line—they owed a considerable amount of money to Mr. Perry's bank. And so it came to pass in the next election, Kershaw seceded from Kershaw County, redrew the county line, and became part of Lancaster County.

Shortly thereafter, Edisto Beach began to have some of the same issues with Charleston County as Mr. Perry and his associates had experienced. The primary issue was that Charleston County stretched from Awendaw to Edisto Beach, more than eighty miles by road. Therefore, as a mostly geographical issue, the residents of Edisto Beach had come to feel neglected. Ergo, they jumped through the identical hoops, and armed with their own petition, seceded, so they could become part of Colleton County. A reasonable person, looking at these events from an objective point of view, would have to conclude that secession is probably a genome in South Carolina's DNA.

★ ★

Shooting Stars over South Carolina
Columbia

Travelers to South Carolina's capital city, Columbia, quickly notice that nearly all roads lead to the center of the city and converge at South Carolina's imposing Greek Revival State House. This crossroads of legislation and history has a background as romantic and dramatic as the state itself. Work began on the Capitol building as early as 1851, but the architect hired for the project succumbed to fraud and dismissal, and a redesigned version was undertaken for the site in 1855. The

Battle scars from 1865

Civil War intervened and slowed the progress, and work was completely suspended in 1865.

It was this unfinished structure at Gervais and Assembly Streets that General Sherman's raiders encountered on February 17, 1865, in their infamous assault on Columbia. This quintessential symbol of Secessionist South Carolina escaped the fires that consumed most of the city, but it was an irresistible target for Yankee artillery. It wasn't until 1903 that the building itself was completed, and the business of the state finally found a home within its granite walls. The copper-domed building is beautifully restored today, but anyone visiting the site can still see the pockmarks from Union cannon fire defacing some exterior walls. Each mark is proudly commemorated with a bronze star. When visiting Columbia, children and historians alike enjoy locating those six stars that recall the grim days at the end of the Civil War. Visit www.scstatehouse.gov for more information.

The Hiss-tory of the *Best Friend*
Columbia/Charleston

Charleston has many famous firsts, including laying claim to America's first regularly scheduled railroad. Construction began in 1828 when news from England reached the ears of city fathers of a successful steam locomotive working there. Locally, the original goal was to build a rail line from Charleston to Hamburg, South Carolina, a fantastic distance of 135 miles. When finished the enterprise would revolutionize trade between the port city and inland markets. The first leg of track was laid between Line Street on the upper Peninsula and Dorchester Road. Even as the tracks were being laid, the technology of steam locomotion was still not well understood. One design was to default to the tried and true power of the wind. On March 20, 1830, a four-wheeled cart equipped with a sail was set atop the tracks near the Line Street terminal.

According to the *Charleston Courier*, "Fifteen gentlemen got on board and flew off at the rate of 12 to 15 miles an hour." Not far up the track however, "The mast went by the board with the sail and rigging attached, carrying with them several of the crew." This experiment was cause for great sport and amusement among the crowd of observers on hand. Wind power was never seriously considered again.

Another reliable power source was tried—the horse. A car was actually built that employed a horse walking on a treadmill. The vehicle was propelled by a series of gears connected to the axles. They dubbed it the "Flying Dutchman." This didn't fly either.

In the summer of 1830 construction of the first steam locomotive began, commissioned by the South Carolina Canal and Rail Road Company. It was manufactured in New York City and shipped in pieces to Charleston by boat. It was named the *Best Friend* by enthusiastic local investors anxious to see it succeed. By Christmas Day of 1830 the *Best Friend* was ready for its debut in a scheduled run along the tracks laid to date, a distance of six whole miles. The smoke-belching locomotive and tender were attached to two "pleasure cars" filled with excited passengers. The *Charleston Courier* recounted the scene:

> The 141 persons flew on the wings of the wind at the speed of fifteen to twenty-five miles per hour, annihilating time and space . . . leaving all the world behind. We darted forth like a live rocket, scattering sparks and flames on either side—passing over three salt water creeks hop, step, and jump and landed all safe before any of us had time to determine whether or not it was prudent to be scared.

Only six months into the railroad's operation, the train was idle at one of its stops while the boiler held a full head of steam, and the escape valve was hissing loudly under the hot South Carolina sun. Annoyed by the irritating noise, the engineer instructed someone to tie off the valve with a handkerchief to stop the nagging problem. This caused the boiler to explode, killing one fireman and badly scalding the engineer. This was only a temporary setback to the rapid

The life-size replica of the *Best Friend* is almost cartoon-like, but it actually runs.
IMAGE FROM ORIGINAL COURTESY OF THE SOUTH CAROLINA STATE MUSEUM, COLUMBIA, SC

expansion of railroads: a small step for the *Best Friend* but a giant leap for rail transportation in America.

A full-scale replica of the *Best Friend* can be seen at the South Carolina State Museum at 301 Gervais Street in downtown Columbia. Call (803) 898-4921 or visit www.southcarolinastatemuseum.org.

★ ★

The Inside Scoop
Columbia

Childhood is a vast wonderland of mysteries and discovery. One of the goals of the EdVenture Children's Museum in Columbia is to explore and celebrate childhood itself. Housed in a building next to the South Carolina State Museum on Gervais Street is an unexpected curiosity for youngsters and adults alike. Just inside the front doors, visitors encounter "the World's Biggest Kid." They call him EDDIE©, and he's a forty-foot-tall, seventeen-and-a-half-ton figure of a seated child. He's made of reinforced plastic, and he physically exemplifies the diversity of South Carolina's children. Outwardly he is the picture of a normal, healthy ten-year-old boy. His T-shirt, baseball cap, and giant tennis shoes are as realistic as they are oversized.

The amazing thing about EDDIE is—you can go inside him. You can climb his vertebrae into his brain, crawl down through his heart, bounce around in his stomach, and (yes, it happens) slide out through his intestines. The journey through EDDIE is a fun way for kids to visualize the inside of their own bodies and understand in a fundamental way how they work.

But EDDIE isn't all there is to EdVenture Children's Museum. There are also 350 individual hands-on exhibits—each one unraveling the mystery of a child's world in a different way. For instance the "World of Work" is explored through a child-size fire truck in a mini-firehouse, a kid-size farm tractor busy in the field, and a kid-size grocery store where little shoppers can buy food for their imaginary dinner. There are also eighty-five thousand square feet of fascinating, educational opportunities in six exhibit galleries plus two outdoor spaces.

The audience for EDDIE and all his surrounding wonders is intended to be universal. But the museum is specifically targeted for children age twelve and younger, and anyone who is a kid at heart. The EdVenture Children's Museum is at 211 Gervais Street, Columbia. Visit www.edventure.org or call (803) 779-3100 for more.

Parents: Be prepared to answer your
kids' questions about where they sell
shoes big enough for EDDIE's feet.

★ ★

"Gentlemen, Start Your Engines"
Darlington

South Carolina has more than its share of fans who follow the fast-growing and lucrative world of NASCAR (National Association for Stock Car Auto Racing). That may be due to the fact that South Carolina is also home to Darlington Raceway, built in 1950 on a shoestring

A temple to fenders, chrome, and squealing tires
GETTY IMAGES FOR DARLINGTON RACEWAY

in Darlington to offer fans an alternative to the high-tech Indy-style racing coming out of Indiana.

Stock car racing was still a fledgling sport when in 1965 the Darlington Raceway president, Bob Colvin, agreed to open a museum similar to the one that opened just off the brickyard at Indy. He'd seen how Indy's museum interpreted the entire history of the sport and the track that had witnessed so much of that history. And by now Darlington and stock car racing had made a history of their own.

Today it is a deeper, richer, and more comprehensive reflection of the passion, courage, and talent that has brought NASCAR into the forefront of America's sports scene. For instance visitors have the opportunity, up close and personal, to see a collection that includes Richard Petty's 1967 Plymouth that won ten races in one fantastic year. Fans enjoy seeing the trademark blue chassis and its bold #43 on the door. They also get to see Darrell Waltrip's 1991 Chevy Lumina, which was involved in one of the most spectacular dust-ups in the history of the sport at the 1991 Pepsi 400. They even have the all-time most-winning stock car on record, the 1956 Ford convertible which won twenty-two titles in a single year plus three additional races the same year with the top welded in place.

The rear of the building features the National Motorsports Press Association (NMPA) Hall of Fame, which includes photos, memorabilia, and hands-on exhibits that illuminate the racing story of NASCAR and many of the personalities that have helped to make it great. One of the most poignant exhibits is the haunting handprints cast in concrete belonging to Dale Earnhardt Sr., who was a nine-time champion of the track, second on the all-time win list of NASCAR drivers.

Whether you're just getting into the NASCAR scene, or you're an old timer looking for where the history was made, the Darlington Raceway Stock Car Museum is worth the pilgrimage to see it. The Museum is at 1305 Harry Byrd Highway in Darlington. Call (843) 395-8821 or visit www.darlingtonraceway.com for hours and directions.

★ ★

Cold War Fallout
Florence County

For the generation who remember "Duck and Cover" as a survival drill for the very real nuclear threat that permeated the 1950s, this story has special resonance. The Cold War was red hot, and everyone was leery of Communist plots and Soviet aggression. The atomic genie was out of the lamp, and the concept of Armageddon was a reasonable fear.

This anxiety really came into focus on March 11, 1958, when a U.S. Air Force B-47 bomber flying over South Carolina en route to England accidentally dropped an atomic bomb. It fell onto a quiet community called Mars Bluff in eastern Florence County. The bomb's plutonium core did not detonate, but the 7,600 pounds of TNT (included with the bomb) exploded, creating a thirty-five-foot by seventy-foot crater, twenty-five feet deep. The explosion destroyed the family home of Walter Gregg, damaged the Mizpah Baptist Church nearby, and cracked walls and rattled windows within a five-mile radius. As the Greggs' daughter later recalled: "We were playing in the yard . . . and suddenly there was a loud noise, like a crash and the next thing we knew dirt and pieces of trees, pieces of the house . . . were falling on us."

No one was killed, but the horror of what might have been haunted the locals for years. On the fiftieth anniversary of the event a commemorative ceremony was held at the site, and the near miss of that day in 1958 was revisited with a combination of awe and thanksgiving.

Test Your Testosterone
Gaston

When it comes to consummate tests of strength, stamina, and the gritty determination to survive seemingly insurmountable physical challenges, it's a good bet someone has called in the Marines. That's the idea behind what is called the USMC Ultimate Challenge Mud Run held twice a year in Gaston near Columbia. It is organized by the Greater Columbia Marine Foundation as a fundraiser in support of local

Marines (and their families) who have been wounded or killed while on active duty. As for size, and it *does* matter, this is the largest Mud Run in North America. One recent count has it that more than fourteen thousand men and women participated in the event divided into 3,600 teams of four competitors. Mud runners compete in different categories according to their age, sex, and physical prowess. There's a corporate version, a coed division, and a pollywog competition for small fry, among others. Participants train for this event for weeks if not months and dress in mud friendly clothes during the competition. Less is more when it comes to Mud Run fashion as overdressed participants can accumulate several extra pounds of mud by the end of the run.

The course itself, called "The Leatherneck," is 5.2 miles in length with more than thirty separate obstacles between the starting point and the finish line. Every challenge has an iconic name from the distinguished history of the Marine Corps. Perhaps it inspires the runners to face an obstacle named for WWII's Mount Suribachi where the Marines raised our flag over Iwo Jima. Maybe runners get an extra push over a fifteen-foot wall when it's built along something called the Ho Chi Minh Trail. And maybe crawling through the A Shau Valley is more doable knowing the Marines crawled through the real thing a generation earlier.

So if you think you've got the right stuff and can outlast the hard core who do this kind of thing for a living, then tell it to the Marines. Show up at the Mud Run and plunge in for all your worth. Visit www.usmcmudrun.org or call (803) 451-1197 for details and registration requirements.

Super-Size "Southern Sequoias"
Hopkins

Most Americans know about the majestic redwood trees out in California's Sequoia National Park. On the other hand few know that South Carolina has its own version of otherworldly giant trees growing along the Congaree River outside of Columbia. The wilderness area

A giant forest still challenges one's
grasp on reality.

✹ ✹

called Congaree National Park contains twelve thousand acres of the largest contiguous area of old-growth, bottomland, hardwood forest remaining in the United States.

Instead of California redwoods this forest is made up of bald cypress, loblolly pine, American beech, water hickory, sweet gum, laurel oak, persimmon, overcup oak, American holly, and swamp chestnut oak. Around thirty of these trees so far have qualified to be called "champions" of their species. The judging of champions is a systematic process where large trees are compared to one another for largest size based on circumference, height, and average crown spread.

How is it that these mammoth trees have survived aggressive harvesting inflicted on them by the logging companies who have swept through the area since the 1880s? The answer is that a soggy wetland area like the Congaree was inhospitable to heavy logging machinery used at the time. The trees with easy access were the first to go. The area also benefited from timely favors procured by a few late-nineteenth-century and, later, mid-twentieth-century conservationists.

Be advised: Walking up to a champion cypress can be hard on a fragile ego. It can be disconcerting to compare oneself to this giant living entity. The feeling is nothing short of a Lilliputian complex. The sweet gum may rise fifteen stories above the ground, and the loblolly pine has been known to soar seventeen stories high. In addition to the fascination of the trees' size and setting, the entire landscape is essentially untouched by man just as it was when Native Americans lived and hunted here. It looked the same when European explorers entered the area for the first time, and it was left standing in place by settlers who filtered through the state on their way west to build a new nation.

Call (803) 776-4396 or visit www.nps.gov/cong for more information.

Just So You'll Know . . .

The mascot for the University of South Carolina's athletic teams is the Gamecock—perhaps an odd choice at first glance. The name comes from General Charles Cornwallis, commander of British forces during the American Revolution, who used the term to describe his adversary, General Thomas Sumter. Cornwallis called him "the Gamecock, because he had the qualities of a fighter who, though worsted, would renew the combat the instant he recovered from the blow."

Gamecock merchandise allows fans to strut their stuff.

Prelude to the Gold Rush
Kershaw

"Carolina gold" is a phrase laden with meaning and promise for South Carolinians. In fact, for us it has several meanings. There was a time when Carolina gold was the rice grown on vast South Carolina plantations that fed the world. Later there were thousands of fields of golden tobacco leaves that were cured and sold for consumption in millions of cigarettes and other tobacco products. Then there was another kind of Carolina gold: the precious ore that has been sought after by mankind since ancient times.

Little known to most Americans is the story of South Carolina's gold rush, which happened decades before gold was discovered in California. The first golden nugget was found in the Piedmont section of the Carolinas in 1799 on land that is now a part of North Carolina. But the gold rush for South Carolina really began in earnest when miners first panned the banks and bottoms of a mill creek in Lancaster County in 1827. The success of these panning efforts opened the floodgates to hopeful prospectors, who filed claims in fifteen other counties in the Upstate. At one time more than one hundred working gold mines were operating in South Carolina. Not all of them paid off, but enough of them did, and by the 1830s gold was the state's second largest industry after agriculture.

One of the most consistently productive mines was on land owned by Colonel Benjamin Haile, and mining operations in that area have been known as the Haile Gold Mine ever since. Ownership of the land has changed many times, and many mining companies have hung out their shingle there, with varying levels of success. At one time gold from this mine financed the Confederate war effort, making it an attractive target for General Sherman when he cut his destructive swath through South Carolina in 1865. He burned all the mine's buildings and equipment, and it remained idle for a dozen or so years. New York investors tried again in the 1880s and brought new technology to the mining process. By the end of the century, the Haile Gold Mine was the most famous and successful producer of gold east of the Mississippi.

The 1970s brought new life to the (by now) played out mine when the price of gold soared to such heights that new mining technologies were developed and brought into play. This revitalized the Haile Gold Mine once more. By the 1990s everyone thought the Haile Gold Mine's profitable days were over, and its luck had finally run out. But the market is a fickle and fascinating thing. In 2010 the price of gold went through the roof and under the guidance of Romarco Minerals, the Haile Gold Mine reawakened once more. Their development investment of $300 million says the company's optimism for the future is nearly unbridled. Investors, stay tuned. Another epidemic of Carolina gold fever may be about to strike.

Discovering South Carolina's Rocky Past
Lancaster County

South Carolina has some geological eccentricities that are worthy of mention. It's not that South Carolinians have a fixation on rocks per se, it's just that the state's landscape is so varied and pummeled by time and history that the weathered carvings of eons long gone have left us with landmarks and destinations of note. There's Caesars Head, a must-see among South Carolina's upstate mountain overlooks, Winnsboro's legendary Revolving Rock, which is said to spin at the sound of loud noises, and Lexington's Peachtree Rock, which contains fossilized sea life from thousands of years ago when the ocean's shoreline was in the Midlands of South Carolina. Perhaps the rarest of all is Forty Acre Rock in the Upstate's Lancaster County.

This rock is not exactly forty acres in size (Southern hyperbole notwithstanding), but, in fact, it is a fourteen-and-a-half-acre flat outcropping of solid bare granite—still darn impressive, even at that size, and holding up nicely after roughly two hundred million years. Tradition says Native Americans once ground their corn in the natural indentations in the rock's surface, and others saw danger and gave names to

South Carolina has a real thing for rocks.

formations in the rock like "Endless Cave" and the "Devil's Footprint." (See "The Devil's Playground," page 242.)

Spring rains fill these indentations creating mini-pools, and these sun-warmed environments become unique habitats in their own right. Modern naturalists have discovered that the rock is a rare and delicate ecosystem, home to sixteen species of plants, twelve of which are endangered. A tiny plant, the pool sprite (*amphiantus*), is known to exist in only five other places in the world. During drought and dry summers these pools dry up, and the rock becomes barren as a desert.

Somehow the seeds manage to hide in the crevices of the rock and leap back into life with the spring rains.

Forty Acre Rock is part of the 1,300-acre Flat Creek Preserve and is not promoted as a tourist attraction due to the fragile nature of its biological habitat. If you visit, tread lightly and expect a moderate hike of about five miles round trip. It is located between Camden and Flat Creek off I-77, at SC 903 and US 601. Call (803) 734-3893 for more information.

Old Hickory's Early Days
Lancaster District

Andrew Jackson, seventh president of the United States, was first a national hero for his leadership of American troops at the Battle of New Orleans against the British in the War of 1812. Known to be both tough and fair, he was called "Old Hickory" by some of his troops, a moniker that stayed with him for the rest of his life. They admired his straight talk and keen judgment. He was also the first presidential candidate to sweep into office on a campaign that proudly touted his humble beginnings, born in a log cabin and raised in a simple way of life. Jackson was acknowledged to be the first president from the frontier, which then meant anywhere west of the colonial states. His colorful life and political career were mostly made in North Carolina and Tennessee, and both states proudly claim him as their own. But the fact remains Andy Jackson owes a lot to the Palmetto State where he was born.

He was born in a place called Waxhaw settlement in the Lancaster District on the North Carolina/South Carolina border on March 15, 1767. He was the third child of Scots-Irish immigrants, but a logging accident claimed the life of his father a few weeks before Andrew's birth. The bereaved mother courageously raised her three sons as best she could as the country inched closer to the Revolutionary War. Jackson was nine years old when the Declaration of Independence was signed, and by the time he was thirteen he enlisted in the Continental

Andrew Jackson's battles in the War of 1812
were nothing compared to the trouble he
has here with local pigeons.
SOUTH CAROLINA DEPARTMENT OF PARKS,
RECREATION & TOURISM

Army. He was running courier messages when he and his brother, Robert, were captured by the British and imprisoned. One day he was ordered to polish a British officer's boots. When he refused in a shocking act of defiance, he was struck by the officer's sword and suffered deep cuts to his hand and head.

Later both Jackson brothers contracted smallpox during their captivity, and Robert succumbed to the disease within days of their release. To add to his grief, Andrew's mother went to Charleston to nurse soldiers convalescing there and soon thereafter died of cholera. Now only fourteen years old, Andrew was alone in the world with little prospect for a bright adulthood. This was the harsh beginning of a future president who found his way to Salisbury, North Carolina, in 1784 to study law. From there it was on to Nashville, Tennessee, and a political career that took him all the way to the White House. Other states may claim him, but South Carolina's hardships groomed him for a life of service to the country he loved. Visit www.southcarolinaparks.com or call (803) 285-3344 for directions and information on Andrew Jackson State Park.

Hunting for the Swamp Fox
Manning, Paxville, Summerton, Turbeville

General Francis Marion, one of the most famous heroes of the American Revolution, was largely famous for being remarkably hard to find. He is said to be the "inventor" of modern guerrilla warfare. The British fought in conventional ways on battlefields and on horseback; by contrast, Marion chose to encounter his enemy in wooded swamps and dense backwaters, which gave him the advantage of surprise attack. The elusiveness of his tactics meant that he had to stay constantly on the move so the British could not find and stop his astonishingly successful band of ragtag rebels. This same elusiveness survived his lifetime and continued through the annals of history until he all but disappeared. So obscure was the image of Francis Marion that when the heroic deeds of the "Swamp Fox" came to the attention of twentieth-century filmmakers, there was little imagery to draw from.

The movie-going public expected a hero as handsome as he was successful in his exploits. The likes of Leslie Nielsen and Mel Gibson played him, and films, stories, poems, and songs were written recounting his stealth and valor, but strangely the true likeness of the man remained in hiding. Maybe that's because the real Francis Marion was

★ ★

The elusive Swamp Fox was finally captured by artists.

short, knock-kneed, hook-nosed, and had piercing black eyes that looked out from a swarthy complexion. Perhaps the heroic accomplishments of the man overshadowed his looks, and he was pushed back into obscurity when famous artists created memorable battle images of Washington, Tarleton, and Cornwallis.

Ironically, glimpses of General Francis Marion can, in fact, be found in an almost hidden trail of outdoor murals displayed in a number of small towns in Clarendon County. At last Francis Marion has come out of obscurity. His likeness appears on the outer wall of banks, shopping centers, and grocery stores. In all, twenty-two murals by different contemporary artists have resurrected scenes from Marion's life and military career. When seen in aggregate, they create a rare, three-dimensional portrait of the famous Swamp Fox from South Carolina. Visit www .swampfoxtrail.com for details on locations and guided tours.

Crazy for South Carolina (and Tennessee)
Marlboro County

A South Carolinian named Mason Lee left an interesting legacy when he died in Marlboro County in 1821. Although he had family, he chose to leave his entire fortune to the states of South Carolina and Tennessee. Poor Mason. He was a bit odd; he'd been struck by lightning as a boy, and thereafter was quite peculiar. He slept in a hollowed out gum tree log for a bed, and he took great pains to avoid women, whom he felt were all witches and evil beings. His curious will was contested by his family with much brouhaha in the late 1820s, and in the final analysis, he was exonerated, and the will was upheld. Amazingly, his legal case is still studied and cited today in decisions concerning mental capacity when executing a will. Go Mason, rock on.

A Different Farmer's Daughter Story
Near Orangeburg

One of the tales to come out of the American Revolution was one about a farmer's daughter, but this one had a different kind of talent: bravery.

The curtain opens on General Nathanael Greene. (He's one of the biggies in the Revolutionary War on our side.) He and his men are in Newberry County at the fork of the Enoree and Broad Rivers. He desperately needs to get a message to his colleague, General Thomas Sumter, who is miles away encamped somewhere along the Wateree River.

The problem is the road from here to there is thick with British soldiers whose sole intent is to intercept any communication between the two. Enter Emily Geiger, daughter of a local farmer, from a plantation nearby. She volunteers to serve her country as a courier, convincing General Greene her womanly wiles might fool the British and actually get the message through. Greene hesitates, but eventually agrees to the plan—she would take his message to Sumter alone.

Emily Geiger's heroism is remembered in this marker
by the old Granby Trading Post.

Exit Emily (on a dark and lonely night). The test for Emily comes when she is halfway to her destination with Greene's urgent message secretly hidden on her person. Curses! The British capture her. (Hiss, Boo.) It seems all is lost and the mission is foiled, except for one thing. Miss Emily has an idea. She quickly reads the message, memorizes it, and then . . . she *eats it*. (Gasp.)

The British find nothing on her person and let her go. Hooray! Emily rides on to General Sumter's camp and recites her message to the commander's startled ears. Her bravery and valor allow General Sumter to join forces with General Greene near Orangeburg and make a redoubled stand against the British. The curtain falls. (Applause.)

Justice at Any Size
Ridgeway

Ridgeway, near Camden in the South Carolina Midlands, has a distinction no other town can claim. They boast of having the world's smallest police station.

It all started back in the days when Fairfield County was in the last throes of the nineteenth-century cotton boom. Farmers still brought their yields to market in mule-drawn wagons and watered their

Ridgeway cut its crime problem down to size.

★ ★

animals at a fountain-fed trough on what is now North Palmer Street (US 21). This central location evolved into an urban hub for other kinds of commerce and activity. By the 1940s Ridgeway required a police force, and one man was hired to do the job. Four walls and a floor were added to the mule watering station, and a police station (of sorts) was born. There was a chair for the officer, a desk for him to work on, a small counter, and one seat for whoever came to call with an injustice, injury, or complaint. That was it.

Somehow, from this closet-sized building, the wheels of justice turned smoothly for fifty years or so until 1990 when, apparently, the specter of vice and crime and mayhem grew to such proportion that the city fathers saw the need to expand their police force. They moved next door, doubling the size of the original police station and doubling the number of people it could accommodate. The old police station was not abandoned altogether; it was rehabbed into the town's bustling visitor center where interesting tidbits of the Ridgeway history and lifestyle are highlighted and promoted to passersby. To find the visitor center, from I-77 take exit 34 onto SC 34 toward Ridgeway. Turn left onto East Church Street (SC 34), then turn left onto North Palmer Street (US 21). The visitor center is on the left. Don't blink or you'll miss it.

When Salley Goes Hog Wild . . .

Salley

It all started innocently enough in 1966 when the town of Salley, South Carolina, (population 410) found itself too poor to buy Christmas lights for the upcoming Yuletide season. It was somebody's idea to stage some kind of festival as a fundraiser, and Salley's incomparable Chitlin Strut was born.

A note to the squeamish: Chitlins are the small intestines of hogs, a Southern delicacy, when washed, boiled, battered, braided, and fried and eaten with unbridled gusto. By all accounts this is an acquired taste. The first hurdle is getting past the smell. They say that during

Salley rises to the occasion each year in time for the Strut.

the festival, usually the Saturday after Thanksgiving, the airspace over Salley is inexplicably void of birds and low-flying aircraft. In the forty-plus years since the festival began, more than one hundred eighty-seven thousand pounds of aromatic chitlins have been rendered up to serve enthusiasts numbering in the tens of thousands. Don't tell anybody, but the demand for pig innards is now such that they've had to go as far away as Virginia to supply the festival's ravenous appetites.

It's not just the morsels of swine anatomy that draw the crowds. It's a festival of local arts and crafts, carnival rides, a parade, and a country music show that sets the scene. Something about the atmosphere seems to be contagious, and attendees get into the spirit with almost religious fervor. There's a Hawg-Calling contest, a beauty pageant with several categories, and a Chitlin Eating contest with world-class competitors of remarkable talent. Best of all is the namesake event for the whole shebang: the infamous Chitlin Strut wherein the contestants (well satiated with chitlins and spirits) compete in a freestyle cakewalk to show how excited they are to be there.

Mark your calendar for late November and make your way to Salley. The interstates have bypassed this little town, but many secondary roads go there. It's roughly twenty-five miles southwest of Columbia. The festival's site address is 258 Pine Street, NW. Visit www.chitlinstrut.com or call (803) 258-3485. Or the other hand, just follow your nose.

Fun by Leaps and Bounds
Springfield

No one knows when frog-jumping contests entered the status of national sport. Mark Twain wrote about it in 1865 when he penned the short story called "The Celebrated Jumping Frog of Calaveras County." In 1928 the setting of Twain's mythical contest actually organized a real one as an official county event. South Carolina hopped on the frog-jumping lily pad in 1967, and the Governor's Frog Jump Contest became an annual event. Various locations hosted the competition, and in 1968 a frog from Springfield took the grand prize and jumped home with the rights to host the contest in Springfield henceforth.

Frog-jumping in Springfield is serious business. Contestants are chosen for their jumping talent in height and distance. Only the most athletically gifted frogs should apply. The field of contestants shows the intensity derived from careful breeding or selection from only the most elite and socially accepted swamps around. One champion leapt into the record books with a flight of eighteen feet, dazzling the crowd and inspiring generations of hopeful tadpoles. The winner is determined after a contestant makes three hops and his accomplishments are measured and certified. The winner goes on to compete for the National Jump-Off held in California's Calaveras County for a $5,000 prize.

**Out-of-season contestants mark time
waiting for their day at the Jump.**

Over the years the contest and its accompanying enthusiasm have spawned additional attractions, making the contest user-friendly for the whole family. Expect to find food, games, carnival rides, street dancing, and a parade where Springfield's finest strut their stuff. Make sure your calendar is open for the Saturday before Easter and start auditioning the best-looking frogs you can find. Come to Springfield and you, too, might be a star. Visit www.springfieldsc.us or call (803) 258-3152.

* *

A Corny Festival—If Ever There Was One

St. George

How it happened is still a matter of conjecture. Some say it dates to the mid-1980s when Bill Hunter, manager of the local Piggly Wiggly supermarket, noticed that his store sold an inordinate amount of grits. When he discussed this fact with his food broker, the suspicion that St. George had a "thing" for grits was confirmed. As it turned out, the population of this sleepy Southern town ate more grits per capita than any other city in the world. This quintessential Southern breakfast staple has grown from a basic side dish of ground corn to a gourmet menu item in high-end restaurants from coast to coast. Not long afterward, St. George's love of grits found expression in a three-day-long festival to celebrate the benefits and wonders of this South Carolina gastronomical favorite. Every April the flags come out, the banners are hung, they start cooking the grits, and the crowds arrive.

Today the World Grits Festival attracts crowds of over forty-five thousand with a parade, a grits queen, and a grits-eating contest. The high point for some comes when a huge vat of grits is prepared, and young people line up to dive in and roll in it. The contestant who leaves with the most grits in or on his person is deemed the winner and subsequently held in high esteem by all in attendance. Bragging rights are enjoyed until next year's event when the entire contest is repeated.

Even though it isn't on every jetsetter's to-do list, the World Grits Festival is lots of fun, and the grits recipes are absolutely fabulous. From I-95 take exit 77 (St. George/US 78) and turn left onto Highway 78. At the second traffic light (about two miles), turn right on Highway 15. The festival site is half a mile ahead, just past the railroad tracks. To check the dates and make appropriate reservations check out the website, www.worldgritsfestival.com.

Where Jiggling and Joggling Is a Good Thing
Stateburg

Any visitor to the urban centers of South Carolina's Lowcountry (Georgetown, Charleston, and Beaufort) will quickly notice our fondness for piazzas. *Piazza* is an Italian word for town square, but in America it means large porch or veranda, and the word's use is especially popular in the Palmetto State. But no piazza is considered complete or well dressed without the addition of a prerequisite joggling board. This curious piece of porch furniture usually consists of a sixteen-foot-long board two inches thick, resting twenty-nine inches high, stretched between two end frames with cross bars. The stanchions sit on rockers that add horizontal movement to the vertical bounce of the board. Children like to ride on this contraption, lovers use it to spoon, bouncing ever closer, and it has rocked generations of babies to sleep for an afternoon nap. According to historians and cultural wags—in the eighteenth century—the joggling board was a whole lot of fun.

The origin of the joggling board has almost entered the realm of legend. Back in the early eighteenth century, a woman on a plantation in Stateburg, South Carolina, was suffering from rheumatism and complained to her relatives in Scotland that she was having trouble getting any exercise. Her concerned relatives sent her a model of a joggling board in hopes that its gentle bounce and relaxing sway would offer some relief. Apparently, joggling boards had appeared on Scottish lawns and in cottage gardens for years. How it worked for the Stateburg plantation lady and her rheumatism is unrecorded, but joggling boards spread like wildfire, and the craze hasn't died out yet.

Until World War II or so they were fairly common in the Lowcountry, but after the war it became difficult to find lumber of the caliber for use in a joggling board, as the wood must be without knots to withstand the rigorous bouncing. But in 1970 the joggling board rode a wave of nostalgia back into the marketplace. The Original Old Charleston Joggling Board Company started crafting the original

★ ★

Ah, to bounce and sway, all night or all day

design by special order. In no time it became a cottage industry, and several other companies have joined the market with their own version of the product. In this day of electronic gadgetry, it would seem that young folks could find other amusements, but joggling boards and piazzas go together like love and marriage, and the jiggle and bounce of a joggling board have lost none of their eighteenth-century capacity to amuse. To learn more call (843) 723-4331 or visit www.oldcharleston jogglingboard.com.

★ ★

One Potato, Two Potato, Three Potato, Four . . .
Sumter

So goes the chant most of us remember from the schoolyard of
our memory, but skipping rope these days has gone way past all
that. Even back then it was rare to see someone successfully Double
Dutch. That was when the jumper negotiated two skip ropes turning

Peculiar Personalities from the Palmetto State

South Carolina is blessed with
an abundance of fun people
who, if the occasion demands
it, can display eccentricities far
beyond the call of expected
behavior. On the national
level, we had Strom Thurmond
and Fritz Hollings as United States senators. Strom's love of the
ladies was legendary, and the media's attempts to understand Fritz's
Charleston brogue certainly met the eccentric test. Every small town
in South Carolina boasts a few of these folks, and the names that
come to mind, "Cussin'" John Bowers and "Bad Eye" Rollins, are
self-explanatory examples. Then there's "Moses," who graces the
streets of Beaufort. No one knows his real name. He gets on his bike
and peddles the streets of Beaufort dressed as Moses, periodically
preaching to anyone that will listen.

Winnsboro had a great character named "Anvil Head." Anvil
Head's entrance into the world was assisted by a midwife who, quite
heavy-handedly, used some forceps and apparently gripped and
pulled too hard. So it came to pass that Anvil Head grew up with
a head that was exceedingly narrow, but exceedingly long. As you
might expect, one eye looked to the left and the other to the right.

simultaneously in opposite directions, which required another whole level of skill. Tradition says Double Dutch jump rope dates back to New Amsterdam before it was called "New York," but Double Dutch as a competitive sport is a late bloomer. Serious competition began in the 1970s in New York City, but its instant popularity made it quickly spread throughout the globe.

Anvil Head found the perfect occupation. He worked at the Amoco station, pumping gas, and checking oil for customers. Anytime there was a new customer, the whole station would turn out to watch him at work. He would invariably come back to the driver side window, hold up the dipstick, and with one eye on the customer and one eye on the dipstick would pronounce the oil to be "okay." Now that will bamboozle almost anyone.

As Hilton Head Island grew and prospered, the demand for local services increased, and the more unexciting jobs, such as septic tank repair, fell on a fellow from Bluffton named "Barefoot" Malphrus. To his friends or strangers, it was just plain Barefoot. You guessed it. Regardless of the weather, he dressed the same every day: carpenter's overalls and barefoot. His reputation for providing fair and honest service over the years allowed him to corner the market on septic tanks. (You can't make this stuff up.) He would come, rain or shine, and provide relief to the desperate homeowner who had called him. Usually, he would hook his tractor up to the lid on the septic tank, poke the contents with a stick, wipe the stick with his bare hands, and make his diagnosis. The homeowner would usually okay the work and promptly flee the scene. He was once asked by a local newspaper how he managed to deal with the omnipresent odor. He thought for a minute, grinned, and said, "It smells like money to me."

★ ★

When the World Double Dutch Tournament in Sumter gets down to business, it's not about your kid sister's skip rope anymore.
COURTESY OF *THE ITEM*, SUMTER, SC

The Annual American Double Dutch League's World Double Dutch Invitational is now held each June in Sumter, South Carolina, with participants coming from all over the country and several foreign nations. At this level the act of skipping rope is now enhanced by gymnastics, speed-jumping, and dancing. Jumpers seem to float in the air acrobatically through a windmill of flying rope turning at nearly impossible speeds. Nowadays teams have names like "Lil Divas" and "Dutch Dragons," which says a lot about how seriously all this is taken.

The creative freestyle event is part rhythm, part tumbling, and part raw talent. The results are dazzling for audiences and participants alike as indicated by the spontaneous outbursts of cheers and applause. Double Dutch isn't just for kids anymore. Several divisions open the competition to jumpers of every age. In Sumter the entry level is third grade. There's a division for junior high school, high school, and college. There's even one for seniors.

The game we called "jump rope" as kids has taken on a new identity and seriousness as shown by its expanding popularity around the world. What's next? Double Dutch for Olympic gold? For more information and tournament schedules go to www.sumtercountysc.org/department/recreation/jumprope.htm.

"Be Careful What You Throw Away"
Sumter

This is not the theme song of a group called "Hoarders Anonymous," but it's a good idea for a song about Swan Lake Iris Gardens. That's how it started—throwing out the trash. Let's start at the beginning.

The year was 1927. Mr. Hamilton Carr Bland, a Sumter businessman, owned thirty acres of land on the outskirts of town near a swamp, not far away from today's West Liberty Street. He was an amateur horticulturalist who wanted to landscape his new home with traditional as well as some unusual flora. Among the plantings were all the standard landscape plants plus some exotic Japanese iris bulbs, which were something of a risk in this setting. Season after season the irises failed to produce their showy blooms. Mr. Bland's lack of success with these iris bulbs had grown to the level of frustration, and he consulted experts in New York. And even they couldn't solve his problem. In disgust he had his gardener unearth the Japanese iris bulbs wherever he had planted them and throw them away. "Away" turned out to be the nearby swamp—where the boggy environment was exactly what the irises had wanted all along. The following spring all the irises

Swan Lake Iris Gardens offers the people of
Sumter quiet beauty all year long.

gratefully burst forth in spectacular bloom, and the seed of Swan Lake
Iris Gardens was planted.

Today visitors are dazzled by more than the magnificent irises in
the expanded 120-acre public park. They also find a large collection of
graceful swans gliding about the cypress trees and on the nearby lake.
In fact every species of swans known in the world is represented here.

★ ★

You'll see some Australian black swans that are descendants of the original ones brought here by Mr. Bland in the late 1920s.

The Sumter Iris Festival is Memorial Day weekend, which catches the full color and bloom of the irises at their spectacular peak. The three-day celebration is a happy marriage between the horticultural beauty and nature's performance on Swan Lake. For a complete schedule of the state's oldest continuously held festival, visit www.irisfestival.org or call (800) 688-4748 or (803) 436-2640.

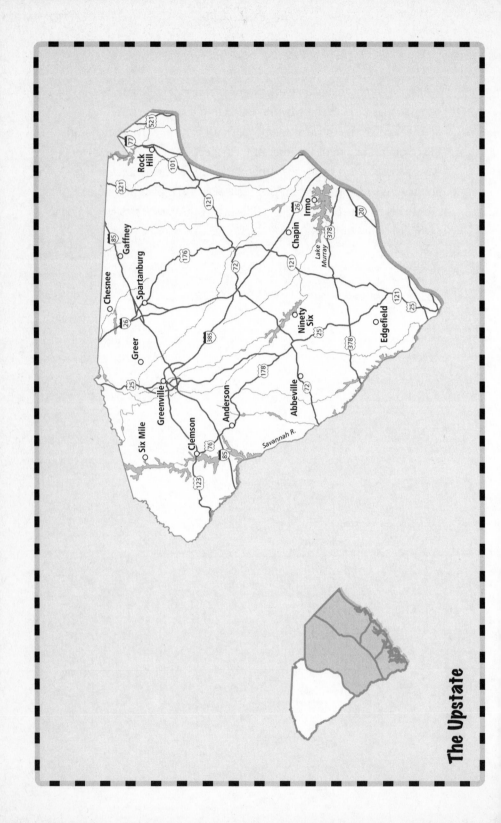

The Upstate

5

The Upstate

The Upstate is *also referred to as the Upcountry, which is also called the Uplands, which is also referred to as the Piedmont. That's too confusing, so for our purposes we'll define it as the upper third of the state that begins in the rolling meadows above the Midlands and changes into the rocky foothills of the Blue Ridge Mountains. The cities of Greenville and Spartanburg lend their urban charms to this area and hold their own against the state's other more famous towns. Then the Upstate goes on to encompass the ghostly, blue mountains themselves, rising some 3,500 feet into the South Carolina sky. The land holds many secrets and memories of historic events.*

Here you'll find important Revolutionary War sites and battlegrounds, like Cowpens and King's Mountain, two decisive victories for the patriots. This area was witness to the evolution of South Carolina's textile industry. There's a Dark Corner to the Upstate where time stood still, and the conventional rules of modern society didn't filter in for several generations. The Upstate is a land of entrepreneurs with dreams as big as Detroit and baseball players whose legends will never die. Here an old Esso station can be caught in a time warp of sixty years and never bat a windshield wiper. And this is where politicians grow as thick as some counties grow corn. That's what makes harvest time in the Upstate so interesting. If you wander up that way, the fields will be calling to you.

★ ★

Abbeville's Strange Anonymity
Abbeville

There are a few names of towns or places that are indelibly and forever associated with great events in America's War Between the States. Harper's Ferry, Appomattox, Gettysburg, and of course Fort Sumter, are classic examples. The town of Abbeville does not ring a bell for most Americans, and yet, Abbeville has been called "the birthplace and deathbed of the Confederacy." Ironically, Abbeville is one of the few towns in the state that escaped actual battle and survived the war largely unscathed.

The place most associated with the creation of the Confederacy is Charleston, where the Ordinance of Secession was signed and read to cheering throngs from the balcony of the Mills Hotel on Meeting Street. However, one month earlier on November 22, 1860, Abbeville hosted the initial meeting where seceding from the Union was the principal topic of discussion, and the plans for secession were first made. The meeting site was on a hill now called Secession Hill, which today is marked with a plaque commemorating the event. This fact is what substantiates Abbeville's claim to be the birthplace of the Confederacy.

A similar misunderstanding exists concerning the technical end of the Confederate government. By the spring of 1865, the Confederacy was in a state of chaos and shambles. On April 18, Mrs. Jefferson (Varina) Davis, wife of the President of the Confederacy, fled Richmond, Virginia, and stopped in Abbeville to stay as a guest of an old family friend, former congressman Armistead Burt. She was followed by a wagon train supposedly laden with the remaining gold from the Confederate treasury. On May 2, two days after Mrs. Davis's departure, President Davis himself arrived in Abbeville accompanied by his cabinet members and guarded by the remnants of five cavalry brigades that constituted what was left of the Confederate government at the time. They stopped at Mr. Burt's home for one night and held what is said to be the last meeting of the war cabinet, where they made the decision to end armed resistance and cease hostilities against the North. This event in the front

THIS MEMORIAL
WAS ERECTED BY
ABBEVILLE CHAPTER
UNITED DAUGHTERS OF THE CONFEDERACY

TO COMMEMORATE THE FIRST ORGANIZED MEETING ADVOCATING THE RIGHT OF A STATE TO SECEDE FROM THE UNION.

THIS MEETING WAS PRESIDED OVER BY THOMAS C. PERRIN, WITH JUDGE D. L. WARDLAW, JOHN A. CALHOUN, DR. J. W. HEARST, JOHN BROWNLEE, DR. J. H. LOGAN AND J. FOSTER MARSHALL, VICE-PRESIDENTS; JAMES C. CALHOUN AND G. McDUFFIE MILLER, SECRETARIES; A. M. SMITH, W. M. ROGERS AND J. F. LIVINGSTON, MARSHALS OF THE DAY.

AFTER PRAYER BY REV. NORTH, ADDRESSES WERE MADE BY: HON. THOMAS C. PERRIN, HON. A. C. McGRATH, GEN. MILLEDGE L. BONHAM, SAMUEL McGOWAN, JAMES N. COCHRAN AND WILLIAM C. DAVIS.

EDWARD NOBLE INTRODUCED RESOLUTIONS OF SECESSION, WHICH WERE ADVOCATED BY THOMAS THOMSON AND UNANIMOUSLY PASSED.

THOMAS C. PERRIN, EDWARD NOBLE, JOHN A. CALHOUN, THOMAS THOMSON, JOHN H. WILSON, D. L. WARDLAW WERE NOMINATED TO REPRESENT THE DISTRICT AT THE CONVENTION CALLED BY THE LEGISLATURE.

NOVEMBER 22, 1860.   NOVEMBER 22, 1927.

"WE HAVE KEPT THE FAITH."

This modest plaque marks the site where secession
was decided and catastrophe ensued.

parlor of what is now called the Burt-Stark Mansion is the place in Abbeville where the Confederate government officially died.

Abbeville's claim on Civil War history is undeniable, but the role Abbeville played in that history remains largely unheralded today. Visit www.burt-stark.com or call (864) 366-0166 for information about tours of the mansion.

A Job for Radio Man
Anderson

James Robert "Radio" Kennedy has an unusual job. He's head cheer-leader, team manager, honorary assistant coach, and official good luck charm for the T. L. Hanna High School Yellow Jackets. Born in 1947, the boy entered his teenage years speechless and mentally challenged. His only companion was a transistor radio he carried in his pocket, which provided a friendly voice any time he needed one.

One afternoon in 1963 the Anderson High School football team was scrimmaging on the school practice field when the boy started hanging around watching the team at play. The coach noticed the boy called Radio and included him in the practices. In his new role as a mascot for the Yellow Jackets, he flourished and his sunny disposition blossomed. Subsequent teams at the school welcomed his participation and even Hollywood came to call. The 2003 movie *Radio* starred Ed Harris as the coach and Cuba Gooding Jr. as Radio. The heartwarm-ing story of James Robert Kennedy continues to this day. Now in his sixties, he's still on the job cheering on the T. L. Hanna High School athletes to be their very best. There's even a bronze statue honoring Radio erected on the school campus near the football stadium at 2600 N. Highway 81 in Anderson.

This statue of Radio in the T. L. Hanna schoolyard reminds students of his spirit on a daily
basis. There's no word if his radio works
or if there's too much static in the air.

★ ★

The Spark of Success
Anderson

For every technological breakthrough somebody has to be first. There are towns that lay claim to the first automobile, the first train, and the first steam engine, but one town in South Carolina stepped up and became the first city in the South whose principal industry was powered by an unending supply of electricity. Anderson, South Carolina, became known as "The Electric City" by the 1890s, and it still carries that moniker today.

It all started when Anderson engineer William Whitner discovered that electrical power could be transmitted by wire from its

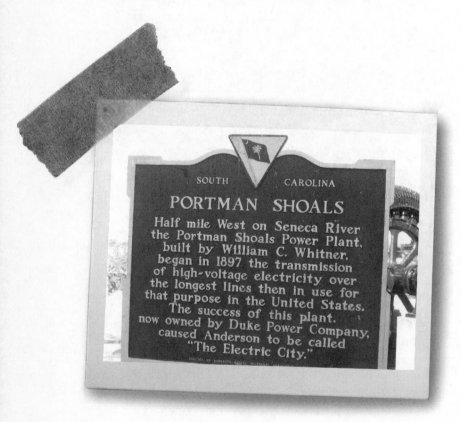

Victorian-era Anderson had a "shocking" reputation.

water-powered source to a nearby textile mill. Soon thereafter the idea spread, and the first electrically powered cotton gin began operation in Anderson County in 1897. This opened the door for hydroelectric power to sweep through the Upstate and spawn the giant textile industry that flourished in South Carolina for more than a hundred years.

History Makes a Touchdown

Anderson

A grassy strip of land outside of Anderson was intended to serve as an emergency landing field for early aviators flying over South Carolina.

(Continued on page 234)

Amelia Earhart paused on her touchdown in Anderson on November 14, 1931, to pose with local dignitaries.

The Brown Bag State

South Carolina has a huge population of Baptists. Because they vote, a significant amount of tortured legislation is routinely passed that appeases this bloc. Most people think the only thing different about Baptists is their preference for total body immersion when they get baptized. The real difference, of course, is they have a clear understanding not to recognize each other in the liquor store.

And so it came to pass that this huge voting bloc was publicly opposed to the repeal of prohibition way back in the 1930s. Although liquor by the drink was available in every other state, we passed the Brown Bag Law in the late 1960s. If a restaurant or a country club had a Brown Bag License, patrons were allowed to carry their own booze into these establishments, provided it was kept out of sight in a brown bag. No kidding! This was a profit bonanza for the clubs in that they could charge $2 for the setup (sodas with ice by the glass for mixing), which was almost pure profit. More importantly, when the monthly bill came, it was listed as *beverage*, so it could be written off. Every country club in the state had a brown bag locker room so that the members would not have to haul booze in and out of the club.

The Baptists were happy, the merchants and clubs were happy, but the state was losing out, because they could only tax the bottle. With everybody happy, of course the legislature could not wait to screw it up. Moreover, since Charleston has always danced to a different drummer, there were copious numbers of open bars freely operating in the city.

To quell the ire of the mostly Greenville-based Baptists who were railing against Charleston's wicked ways, the governor decided to send the state's law enforcement division, SLED, to raid the Charleston bars. As a courtesy, SLED called the Charleston police chief to say that they were coming. The police, in turn, notified the mayor, who was having a drink at the time in one of the bars. Striking quickly, the mayor told the police chief to have the SLED raiders arrested. As time wore on, and the governor had not heard from the SLED team, he called the mayor of Charleston and inquired as to whether he knew anything about their disappearance. The mayor replied, "I know exactly where they are. They are in my jail. If you will go the bail, I'll let 'em out!"

The Baptists, the legislature, and the governor were, of course, incensed that such things could occur, so they created some of the most nonsensical liquor legislation to come out of any state in decades. The legislature did away with the Brown Bag Law and replaced it with the Mini Bottle Law. It was now legal to drink in bars and country clubs provided the booze was poured from a 1.5-ounce bottle that carried a 75 cent liquor stamp. There were massive restaurant closings, and many country clubs that had counted on their bar to pay for golf course fertilizer found themselves up the creek. Heck, it even caused an illegal casino in Charleston to close . . . but at least the Baptists were happy, and the state had a new income source. Hallelujah, amen.

★ ★

(Continued from page 231)

It later became a regular stop on the air mail route across the state, but it wasn't really consecrated until November 14, 1931. That's when Amelia Earhart, America's "first lady of the skies," touched down here in an Autogiro. The gangly aircraft (an early version of a helicopter) was a rare sight at the time and drew large crowds for its sponsor, Beechnut chewing gum. Shortly after this brief visit to Anderson, Ms. Earhart made her world-famous solo flight across the Atlantic from Newfoundland to Ireland on May 20, 1932. A plaque at the site of the former airfield denotes Ms. Earhart's visit, but the details have faded into the mists of time as has the wistful Amelia Earhart herself.

South Carolina Fast Food
Chapin

From June through late August, just off Amick's Ferry Road slightly west of Chapin, the Shealy family has just about the best vegetable garden and stand around. When you drive up, you quickly notice that no one is in sight. All the vegetables are beautifully laid out: okra, tomatoes, string beans, butter beans, peaches, and the list goes on and on. What you do see is a series of signs telling you to HELP YOUR-SELF, what every item costs, and to PUT YOUR MONEY IN THE OLD AMMO CAN nailed to a nearby post. On any given day, you might see four or five folk waiting on themselves, weighing the produce, and putting their money in the ammo can.

The signs make the place. Last, but not least, is our favorite: CHILDREN, DO NOT PET THE OLD BLACK DOG. HE IS OLD AND CRANKY AND WANTS TO BE LEFT ALONE.

This is the honor system's cash register at
Shealey's Vegetable Stand.

Dining with Peggy Sue
Chesnee

Get out your poodle skirt and your saddle oxfords. This is South Carolina's take on a 1950s-themed restaurant that really rocks your socks.
We're talking about a restaurant built and dedicated to a beloved time
and its dynamite music, not a homogenized, all-purpose franchise
model. Meet and fall in love with Bantam Chef Restaurant, located
three miles south of the North Carolina line on US 221 in the small
town of Chesnee. This is David and Sandra Walker's '50s-style eatery
that's been spinning the oldies and turning out burgers and shakes for
more than forty years.

Cheeseburgers, Studebakers, and rock 'n roll a la carte.

Here's an offering of the drive-in fare and down home meat 'n
three that fed America through the '50s and '60s. The ample breakfast menu includes fresh homemade biscuits and gravy and caricature
pancakes of popular cartoon characters from today and yesteryear.
They turn back the clock by serving a cup of hot, steamy coffee for
only twenty-five cents. The lunch plates are the same as were typical
then as are the burgers, fries, and ice cream that were so loved back
in the *Happy Days*. Remember liver mush, grilled pimento cheese sandwiches, ice cream floats, and old-fashioned malts? How about trying

the Studebaker-A-Plenty or the Carolina Combo? But be sure to bring a huge appetite.

It's not only the food that takes customers back to another time. A memorabilia room is crowded with nearly every '50s collectible available including a 1950 Studebaker, 1958 three-wheeled BMW, and a couple of motorcycles that could have traveled with Marlon Brando in *The Wild Ones*. These are from the owner's private collection of more than 150 vintage automobiles. All of the memorabilia was lovingly collected by the owners, whose genuine affection for the material is obvious and delightfully shared with the public. Hard Rock Café, eat your heart out. This is the real be-bop, a-re-bop, sha-boom. Crash, bang. Visit www.bantamchefchesnee.com or call (864) 461-8403 for more.

Burr under the Saddle
Chester

Once upon a time (actually it was 1807), a mysterious group of men on horseback arrived in the town of Chester, South Carolina. One of the men stood out from the others, because he was tall, well dressed, and wearing shackles on his wrists. Just as the group entered the town square, the shackled man jumped from his horse, broke free of his captors, and leapt onto a nearby rock. He shouted to the assembled crowd at the top of his lungs. Clearly, the man had skills as an orator, because the crowd quickly responded to his ranting and gathered 'round to hear more. As he was berating his guards for their unjust treatment of him, he launched into a diatribe about the evils of the American government. He allowed as how the Southwestern states should reorganize and secede from the Union and form a new country for the specific purpose of attacking and acquiring Mexico. Oh, and by the way, the new country would need a dynamic emperor, and that man should be him.

By this time, the guards had reorganized and regained control of their prisoner. At gunpoint he was physically lifted back onto his saddle, and their journey on to Washington, D.C., resumed. Once

In 1806 Aaron Burr while passing through Chester, a prisoner dismounted on this rock and appealed in vain to the bystanders for help.

An unlikely podium for a politician of note

there he would stand trial for treason and be acquitted. As the men on horseback rode out of town, the people of Chester were somewhat bewildered by this incident. But when the dust settled and the facts came out, they had encountered a brief visit with none other than a Vice-President of the United States of America, Aaron Burr.

★ ★

Raptor Respite En Route to Southern Climes

Cleveland

If you're lucky or you time it just right, a very special treat is waiting for you at Caesars Head State Park in upstate South Carolina.

The right time is mid-fall—September through November—and the scene worth waiting for is a bright, blue autumn sky filled with mighty birds—raptors of every ilk—soaring, swirling, and swooping, organizing themselves for a long journey. This frenzy of feathers and flight is part of their annual migration to Central and South America where the warmer weather sustains them until spring calls them back home. Birdwatchers and nature lovers alike marvel at this noisy convention of magnificent flyers assembled at an elevation of up to 3,200 feet. You'll see hawks, falcons, eagles, kites, and more sharing the air together. Sightings have included Bald Eagle, Mississippi Kite, Sharp-shinned and Cooper's hawks, Merlin, even Osprey, Turkey and Black vultures. It's not unheard of to see three hundred raptors in the air at one time. The highest day count on record is more than 5,200 birds.

The air show is especially wondrous when seen against the backdrop of Caesars Head itself, in the peak of its bright fall color. This park features a massive granite outcropping atop the Blue Ridge Escarpment. Together with neighboring Jones Gap State Park, they create the Mountain Bridge Wilderness. The two parks contain eleven thousand acres of unspoiled southern mountain forest. While you're on the mountain, be sure to catch some of the other highlights at Caesars Head like the 420-foot Raven Cliff Falls accessible by a suspension bridge that provides the best view. Hiking trails range from easy to difficult, and the higher you go the better your view of the birds.

Caesars Head State Park is located at 8155 Geer Highway in Cleveland. Contact the park interpreter at (864) 836-6115 for more information about the Hawk Watch Program or visit www.southcarolinaparks.com.

Sign of the Times
Clinton

Might as well admit it—South Carolinians have never been shy about expressing their political opinions. This verbosity shows up in all kinds of strange places. Take, for instance, the signage along US 76 in Newberry. During the 1992 and 1996 campaigns for president, drivers heading north did a double-take. The reason was a green highway sign at the intersection of US 76 and SC 219, directing traffic toward two local towns, not too far away. It reads CLINTON and a large arrow points to the right. Another sign says, PROSPERITY, and the arrow points to the left.

If this none-too-subtle advice offends your political sensibilities, simply turn around and approach the intersection from the opposite direction. This approach will advise you Clinton will be on the left, and Prosperity will be found to the right. The South Carolina Department of Traffic and Transportation (SCDOT) has all points of view covered.

Worshipping in the Round
Conestee

The town of Conestee in Greenville County seems an unlikely place to find an architectural jewel. South Carolinians are used to finding these little gems in places like Charleston, Beaufort, and Georgetown, but sitting right in the middle of town is a remarkable structure known as McBee Chapel. It is a rare example of an architectural style briefly popular in America between 1840 and 1860, based on the geometric form of the octagon. There are octagonal barns like the one near York, South Carolina, but McBee Chapel is actually a house of worship, a Methodist Church, built circa 1842.

This particular example was the brainchild of Vardry McBee, an early Greenville industrialist sometimes known as the "Father of Greenville." He paid for it, but credit for the building's creativity goes to a local wheelwright named John Adams. Adams was interested in maximizing the seating space and felt that could be accomplished in a building

Are we talking politics here or what?

shaped like an octagon. (It seats 150.) The octagon provides one-fifth more floor space than does the square with the equal length of wall.

The chapel is constructed of brick and has a pyramidal-shaped roof topped by an eight-sided louvered cupola. The base of the building is skirted by a broad whitewashed band, and there is a cornice of molded brick at the roofline. At one time there was a slave balcony, which has been removed, and the small stained glass windows surrounded by panes of clear glass were added later. No mention is made of brides and grooms getting lost on their way to the altar, but apparently many weddings have occurred in the chapel with no confusion recorded.

To find McBee Chapel at 53 Main Street in Conestee, travel one mile south of SC 291 on US 29, and turn east on Fork Shoals Road into Conestee.

The Devil's Playground

You've heard a lot about South Carolina being in the heart of the Bible belt. It might lead you to believe South Carolinians are essentially a pious people who for the most part follow the straight and narrow path of righteousness. But upon closer inspection you'll discover that South Carolinians have given equal time to the dark side, as they named many of their natural wonders and geological curiosities for the devil himself. You don't have to travel very far before encountering something named for the devil. Apparently at some time or another, the devil cut a wide swath through the Palmetto State.

One example is Devil's Track Rock near Lexington, where early German settlers were deemed to be emissaries from hell for speaking in a foreign tongue. Another is Devil's Kitchen near Caesars Head in Greenville County, which is said to emit smoke and noxious odors whenever Satan is cooking dinner. Speaking of sitting down to a meal, the Devil's Elbows are said to be in Kershaw County, and his Fork has been located in Oconee County (visit Devil's Fork State Park, www.southcarolinaparks.com). The restless devil left his mark on the Forty Acre Rock outcropping in Lancaster County where his footprints have been traced on the granite surface. (See "Discovering South Carolina's Rocky Past," page 202.) But when he wants to go home and hide out until his next mischief, he retreats to Hell Hole Swamp in Berkeley County, a 2,125-acre swamp ideal for a devil's earthly respite. (See "A Good Time in Hell," page 121.) The jury is still out on whether these names were given in fear and trepidation of the devil's revenge, or whether this is a subtle expression of awe and respect at his omnipresent handiwork.

Let's Talk Turkey
Edgefield

South Carolina is home to one of the most amazing rebirth and reestablishment stories of wildlife in the United States. Forty years ago the wild turkey was all but extinct. It had suffered double calamities of loss of habitat and over hunting. It is a known fact that the wild turkey once lost out to the eagle as our national symbol by just a few votes in Congress. Furthermore, every school kid in America has been told of the original Thanksgiving dinner with indigenous Indians in Virginia.

After successful restoration and conservation efforts, turkey hunting began to get some traction in the mid-1980s as they began to proliferate sufficiently to allow some culling. Once hunters began to try to bring one home, they soon realized that this was one smart, wily bird. Every turkey hunter today has at least one story in which this old bird made a perfect fool out of the hunter.

The Winchester Turkey Museum celebrates not only the game bird itself, but the skills required of those who pursue it.

Not only smart, turkeys are beautiful to see particularly when they are "drumming" in full strut. There are subtle differences between the domestic bird, raised to sell at Thanksgiving in the grocery store, and the wild version. The wild bird has a much larger head, bigger waddle, which is the bright red jowl, and long "beards" which are hairlike appendages on the breast of the bird. Interestingly enough, they will allow people in cars to get near them, but flee at the sight of a human. They have extraordinary hearing and eyesight.

The males are hunted in the spring in South Carolina. There are numerous strategies to bring Mr. Tom home for supper. You must know where they hang out. Then, you need to see (or hear) what stand of trees that they choose for a roost. One of the better "locator" calls is the barn owl call. For whatever reason, turkeys just do not like owls and when the "who . . . who . . . whoooo" is given, turkeys will often gobble back. Then there are the call boxes. These boxes are made of wood and a chalked wooden scraping system driven by a rubber band that imitates the subtle "chuckle" gobble of the female turkey. The biology of all known species kicks in, and Mr. Tom will seek out this invitation for a tryst. The last element in the hunting process involves camouflaging the hunter as if he is a sniper. It's a guy thing.

Now that you know the basics, the next step is to visit the National Wild Turkey Federation's Wild Turkey Center and Winchester Museum in Edgefield at 770 Augusta Road. These are the folks who have helped to restore wild turkey populations around the country and to conserve nearly fourteen million acres of wildlife habitat. The museum is a fascinating mix of interactive exhibits and dioramas including the world's largest turkey call as well as a fine collection of historic hand-crafted calls, specimen birds depicted in their natural settings, and even a wildlife oddity exhibit—all telling the story of the wild turkey in America. You may also want to look over their website for more at www.nwtf.org.

A Man Called Dave

Edgefield County

A very large jar which has 4 handles
Pack it full of fresh meats—then light—candles

This simple poem may not qualify for the *Oxford Book of American Verse.* But for its time and in its place, it was beyond imagination, a wonder.

The author of the above poem, written on April 12, 1858, was a slave named Dave. His first owner was a religious man named Harvey Drake who against all mores of the day taught a few of his slaves to read, so they could benefit from studying the Bible. At the time literacy

The tradition of Edgefield pottery is kept alive at Old Edgefield Pottery, where contemporary artisans display and sell their wares.

was forbidden for slaves, as their owners were afraid such knowledge would lead to unrest and revolt. Little more is known about Dave other than the fact that he apparently lost a leg at some time in his early life. As a result of this he was unfit for working in the fields but qualified for a job in a sitting position. His second owner was Dr. Abner Landrum. In addition to his medical practice, he owned a pottery yard. The Landrumsville Pottery had about fifteen slave families who worked at pottery wheels creating high quality, alkaline-glazed stoneware. One of those workers was Dave. Pots, jars, and jugs from this kiln came to be known as "Edgefield District Pottery."

About 1834 Dave began to sign and date the jars he personally created, which was unheard of at the time. Dave's signature pottery became a forum for his thoughts and ideas. He began to inscribe verses, sayings, and biblical phrases on some of his pots. Today, those pots (the ones that have survived) are the poignant autobiography of a man in slavery. It is also a kind of jigsaw puzzle for historians to use in retracing the lives of African Americans post-emancipation. Their strength and beauty are immeasurably augmented by the gentle poetry of a gifted man.

> I wonder where is all my relation
> friendship to all—and every nation
> —Dave, August 16, 1857

Today, Dave Drake's pots are found in the finest museums in America including the Smithsonian Institution. In South Carolina they can be seen in the Charleston Museum and the South Carolina State Museum in Columbia. The Old Edgefield Pottery at 230 Simkins Street in Edgefield is another place where Dave's work (and other slave-made pottery) can be seen along with new pieces by contemporary artisans. On rare occasions a work by Dave will turn up in an auction, and if collectors know about it, the bidding climbs out of sight. A recent find brought $40,000. Visit www.charlestonmuseum.org and www.south carolinastatemuseum.org to learn more.

Something in the Water?

Edgefield County

It's almost a cliché, but *something* is different about South Carolina's Edgefield County. This quiet district in the lower Piedmont area produces an uncanny number of movers and shakers who come under the general category usually known as politicians. For starters a plaque posted in downtown Edgefield brags that ten South Carolina governors came from here. Edgefield was also the birthplace of several military generals, other heroes, and a roster of U.S. representatives and senators that reads like a "Who's Who" in the history of Washington,

Edgefield's distinguished sons are celebrated in signage at nearly every corner.

D.C. One notable example is Strom Thurmond, who served longer in the U.S. Senate than anyone else until 2006. (He retired at age one hundred having served the Senate for forty-eight years.) There was also Jim Bonham, a hero of the Alamo back in 1836.

As to the special properties of Edgefield County water, the results are inconclusive. All tests for unusual amounts of valor, verbosity, venom, and verve have proved negative. The same is true for taints of tenacity, trustworthiness, and basic tact. As far as anyone knows, the water is not the catalyst.

To look for another answer to the political proliferation, follow I-20 to SC 121 toward Trenton, then turn left on US 25 to Edgefield.

All That Business between the Sheets
Fort Mill

The man was named Colonel Elliot Springs. He was already widely known by the American and European press as a World War I flying ace and all-around *bon vivant.* But after the war all that glamour and attention began to fade. About the same time his wealthy father, owner of a now financially precarious textile mill in upstate South Carolina, passed away, leaving the business to his son. War contracts had left Springs Mills overbuilt and monetarily overextended. A huge inventory of bedding was ready for sale, and buyers were hard to find.

Colonel Springs marshaled his eccentric personality and came up with a new way to market these products—by riding in on the coattails of America's relaxing morals, a byproduct of the Jazz Age. In other words, he knew what others didn't know for fifty more years or so—that sex sells.

He launched a daring ad campaign in national magazines utilizing the double entendre for shock value and notoriety. Each ad featured some female American icon in some provocative state of undress with an ardent admirer nearby—very nearby. The headline described a situation or some attribute of Springmaid brand bedding that could easily be interpreted as X-rated, only on closer inspection it was as innocent as a plain white sheet. One example that nearly caused a riot featured an exhausted young Indian collapsed but satisfied in a hammock made of Springmaid sheets. Climbing out of this shared lovers' lair was a buxom Indian maiden looking rather glowing herself. The headline read: "A Buck Well Spent on a Springmaid Sheet." Of course, the copy talked about the dollar value of the Springmaid product, but the ad nearly stopped the presses in mainstream magazines coast to coast.

This was the opening volley of a revolution in marketing textiles for the American home, and nothing could stop Elliot Springs now. In an industry where sheets had been sold separately as flat goods on an open shelf with virtually no distinction between brand names, suddenly Springmaid sheets were exceptional, and people were calling for them by name. Packaging changed. Stripes, solid colors, and pastels were offered. At last, an industry nearly killed by a world war and the Great Depression was back on solid ground.

By the 1980s Springs Mills had grown to a business with annual sales of $917 million. It was one of the state's largest employers and ranked as the fourth largest publicly held textile company in the nation. But once again there was change in the air, and advertising became more sophisticated and very research-oriented. Also, textiles manufacturers from offshore captured the majority of the business, and the southern textile empire all but faded away. But many remember the aggressive and creative marketing of Colonel Elliot Springs, who saved an outmoded Southern industry from a premature death.

The Wrong Right-of-Way
Gaffney

Just 3.8 miles north of the Gaffney "Peach" water tower on I-85 (past exit 95) there's a curiosity that only a politician could love. (See "Gaffney's Peachy Keen Water Tower," page 250.) As negotiations were underway to discern the right-of-way for the new Interstate 85 being planned, there were the usual obstacles and stumbling blocks. Plans were made and properties were bought, slicing through long-held

★ ★

family farms and business sites of every description. Slowly but surely
a viable right-of-way took shape through Cherokee County, until the
planners encountered an apparently immovable object, a nineteenth-
century cemetery. This situation was not unique to road-building in general. What usually happens in such a case is one of two things: Either
the cemetery is moved en masse through an arduous legal and ethical
effort, or the right-of-way is rerouted to avoid the location altogether.

Of course, South Carolina chose another path. In this case they split
the road down the middle. The northbound lanes veered to the right
of the graves, and the southbound lanes stayed to the left. Occupants
of the cemetery were stranded uncomfortably in the center median.
Little or no access was made for visitors to these graves, most of which
date from the 1850s to the 1880s.

The cemetery is only visible as a drive-by curiosity to travelers along
I-85. You have to be sharp-eyed to see it these days as its inaccessibil-
ity has led to benign neglect, and South Carolina's verdant growth
tends to obliterate the site for much of the year. The lesson for politicians and engineers of future South Carolina roads may be this: The
path of least resistance isn't always the right one.

Gaffney's Peachy Keen Water Tower
Gaffney

Georgia makes a lot of noise about those Georgia peaches you've
heard so much about, but the fact is South Carolina grows more
peaches than any other state in the Southeast, and sends these delicious gifts to appreciative palates all over the world. The battle for
bragging rights over who grows more peaches reached new heights
in 1980–81 when the city fathers of Gaffney, South Carolina, commissioned a new water tower to serve their growing municipality.
Designers came up with a giant peach atop a pedestal that dominates
the landscape along I-85 between exits 90 and 92. The giant peachoid
disguises a water tank holding one million gallons—that's lots of
peach nectar. The sixty-foot green leaf sticking out of the peach's stem

Gaffney's water tower has been called a peach on steroids.

weighed seven tons when it was hoisted up atop the tower as a finishing touch to the disguise.

When it was first built artists were hired to paint the sphere to look as much like a peach as possible including a pronounced cleft to show the fruit's natural contours. The finished work, however, was misconstrued by drivers along I-85. They felt it looked like a baby's bum or a giant "moon" to passersby from the people of Gaffney. A hasty repaint required fifty gallons of paint in twenty different colors creating the realistic hues of a peach ripened in the Carolina sun. No word yet from Georgia in rebuttal, but the Gaffney water tower makes a convincing argument that South Carolina's peach crop does in fact reach new heights every year.

By the Light of the Silvery Moon
Gowensville

An ever-shrinking number of old time South Carolinians can remember when covered bridges were fairly common along the backroads and older byways throughout the state. The advent of superhighways and modern bridge engineering have all but erased the covered bridge from the American landscape. In South Carolina there's only one left, and it's in Greenville County near a town called Gowensville. Campbell's Covered Bridge is named after a man who donated the land for its construction and whose nearby grist mill benefited when area farmers had easier access to his place of business. Construction was

Crooning love's tune under a covered bridge.

completed in 1909, and the finished wooden bridge measured thirty-five feet long and twelve feet wide, and looked like a long, red garage with openings at both ends.

Covered bridges like this represented state-of-the-art technology for mountain roads at the turn of the century when ice and snow at streams and crossings could be life threatening to travelers. A dry bridge was a welcome site that ensured a safer passage to an intended destination. Time and weather took their toll, and Campbell's Bridge fell into disrepair like the three others built in Greenville County at about the same time. Campbell's Bridge was spared demolition and underwent a restoration in 1964 and again in 1990. Although it is no longer used for traffic, the bridge is accessible to the public for picnics, hiking, and delightful flights of nostalgia. No doubt, some visitors still recall a time when a buggy or a Model T waited under its roof for a rain shower to pass. And by the light of a silvery moon many a lad stole a kiss in the semi-darkness of this wooden mountain lair. To find it, starting in Greer, head north on SR-14 (N. Highway 14). Turn left on SR-414 (Highway 414) and go 1.1 miles to Pleasant Hill Road. Turn left again on Pleasant Hill Road traveling 0.4 miles, and then turn right on Campbell Covered Bridge Road.

Hairless Peanuts?

Greenville

A man and his wife, from a foreign country (New Jersey), walked into a restaurant on Main Street in Greenville and were promptly seated. The man said to the waitress, "We're from out of town and this is our first visit to South Carolina. We have decided that we would soak up as much of the local flavor as we could, and we would like to know if you have any of those hairless peanuts that I hear everyone talking about?" The waitress replied, "I have lived here all my life and know this state pretty well, but I have never heard of hairless peanuts."

With that, the lady from New Jersey said, "I just heard the people at the next table talking about the bald peanuts!" The waitress broke

★ ★

In season boiled peanut stands spring up like
daisies along South Carolina roadsides.

out in peals of laughter and said to the lady, "That's the way we say
'boiled.'"

So if you have a chance while you are soaking up the local flavor,
try some; or better still, make them yourself. Just get a really big pot;
fill it with "new crop," or green peanuts and water; add at least a
box of salt; and "bal 'em" about an hour or so. Cool them down with
some ice in the pot, pop open a cold one, and you will enjoy something really fine.

Holy Madonna!
Greenville

What a surprise to find a world-class art collection tucked away in a small Christian-oriented liberal arts college in upstate South Carolina. In Greenville on the campus of Bob Jones University, you'll find the BJU Museum & Gallery, said to be one of the finest collections of Italian paintings in America.

The collection was started in 1948 by evangelist/educator Dr. Bob Jones Jr. He felt exposure to great art should be an integral part of higher education at his growing university. He narrowed the criteria for the first purchases to be culturally focused on Western religious art. The original collection consisted of twenty-five Italian paintings and included works by Tintoretto, Botticelli, Veronese, Ghirlandaio, and Ribera. These purchases were made at a time when the market for Baroque religious art was depressed, so Dr. Jones was able to acquire these major works at incredibly low cost. These first paintings would become the foundation for their Old Masters Collection, which grew to include works by Rubens, van Dyck, Gerard David, Cranach, Honthorst, Murillo, and Doré. Together the paintings represent the history of European religious art from the fourteenth through the nineteenth centuries. As the collection grew so did the need for more exhibition space, and the museum moved twice during the 1950s and '60s. At its present location, it contains more than four hundred works of sacred art on permanent display.

In addition to this main collection are several other special exhibits with a religious theme. Among them are "The Progress of Revealed Religion" by Benjamin West—famous English painter of the eighteenth century—and the Bowen Collection of Antiquities, religious artifacts from ancient Babylon, Egypt, Palestine, and Rome. The Russian Icons collection traces the evolution of Russian religious iconography from the fourteenth through twentieth centuries.

To enjoy this "divine" experience for yourself, visit the website for directions, hours, and admission fees at www.bjumg.org or call (864) 770-1306. The university is located at 1700 Wade Hampton Boulevard in Greenville.

★ ★

Don't Hold the Mayo
Greenville

If you make a condiment that pushes aside all the national brand names on the grocery store shelf, then you must have something special. The thing about Eugenia Duke was her contagious enthusiasm. She made sandwiches as an act of love and feeding people at her table was always a joy. This passion for sharing good food started in 1917 when she made sandwiches of roasted meats, fresh breads, and tart mayonnaise for World War I troops passing through Greenville en route to training at nearby Fort Sevier. Some of the guys actually wrote back to her for a jar of mayonnaise to send home to mother. Her sandwiches were also a hit with customers at a local drugstore lunch counter. One cautious grocer allowed her to market a few jars of the mayonnaise in his retail store.

This familiar jar is never far away where
sandwiches are made and enjoyed.

Mrs. Duke's sandwiches were great, but the one thing everyone raved about was her mayonnaise. The recipe had no added sugar or egg-white fillers and used cider vinegar, which gave it a smooth, creamy, slightly tart taste. So distinctive was this mayonnaise that very soon she found it in demand by restaurateurs and chefs throughout the state.

By 1920 Mrs. Duke faced a dilemma. Should she continue supplying sandwiches to lunch counters and corner grocery stores or concentrate on the manufacture of the mayonnaise for a larger customer base? Her decision was to sell the sandwich business and make mayonnaise full-time. By 1923 her new Greenville manufacturing plant started turning out jars of mayonnaise by the thousands as its fame spread throughout the South. This garnered the attention of the Richmond, Virginia–based C.F. Sauer Company, which purchased the business and her recipe in 1929. Her recipe remained unaltered and even the Greenville plant is still in production today. She stayed on with the firm as head of sales until she moved to California to be closer to her daughter. Mrs. Duke died on February 26, 1968, at the age of ninety.

Today, Southerners all know that Duke's Mayonnaise is a necessary staple in every good kitchen. Some customers wouldn't dream of eating a sandwich or making potato salad without it. The shelf space her mayonnaise commands today is testimony to the quality of one woman's product and the stamina of her entrepreneurial spirit.

We Know It Ain't So, Joe
Greenville

When he was born on July 16 in Pickens County back in 1888, there was nothing about this boy that would indicate he would grow up to change the face of baseball forever. Joseph J. Jackson was the eldest of eight children, and his father was a mill worker like so many others trying to eke out a living to feed his family. In 1901 the family moved to the Brandon Community of West Greenville where his father found employment in the textile mill there. Joe was no different from many

In his day, Shoeless Joe's batting average
was as famous as his name.
COURTESY OF THE SHOELESS JOE JACKSON MUSEUM, GREENVILLE, SC

other children of mill workers who worked in the mill to help support their families. This left no time for schooling, so he never learned how to read or write. His situation left little room for Joe to find success—until he found the game of baseball at the age of thirteen. The Brandon Mill baseball team gave him the first chance for real success at something.

Soon enough he was playing for a semi-pro team called the Greenville Spinners. During one of their games against the Anderson Electricians, Joe took off his new spikes, because blisters were irritating his feet. The crowd saw a shoeless Joe hit a triple and dubbed him "Shoeless Joe" Jackson for the rest of his career. He never played shoeless again, but he went on to build an outstanding professional league baseball record.

Fame and fortune and love of the game sometimes bring out the worst in people. In 1919 a gambling scandal surrounding the World Series tinged our Joe and brought a startling end to his brilliant career (although Joe himself was eventually cleared). Afterwards he moved back to the South and finally settled in his hometown, where he operated a number of businesses near the old mill where he first learned the rules of the game. Eventually the modest house he once owned was moved to the edge of Greenville's Fluor Field where baseball fans and historians delight in their visit to the Shoeless Joe Jackson Museum at 356 (numbered to reflect Joe's lifetime batting average) Field Street. Visit www.shoelessjoejackson.org for more information.

Riding High
Greer

Do your driving skills need a little tweak? Is that darned backseat driver on your case? Do your teen drivers scare you to death? Or, are you a Mario Andretti wannabe? South Carolina has an answer for you. And it's the BMW Performance Driving School located in Greer, not far from Greenville. So deep is BMW's love for the driving experience that they invested $12 million in the facility.

On road or off, better driving skills are the goal of
the BMW Performance Driving School.
CHRIS STANFORD

No kidding, you can go to a serious, no-nonsense, professional
driving school for drivers at every level. The goal is graduation, the
standard is excellence, and it doesn't hurt that you'll be driving BMW
vehicles. Isn't *that* nice? You can choose from a one- or two-day program for new performance drivers or those who want a tune-up. More
experienced drivers can sign up for the advanced M School to perfect
their existing driving skills. Teens learn about caution and safety. Even
motorcycle drivers get a chance to enhance their ride. Everybody wins
by learning to know and love the thrill of the driving experience.

★ ★

Learning takes place under the guidance of professional instructors on every possible driving challenge: dry track, wet track, slalom course, and a course called "Other Roads." Imagine the freedom to legitimately, professionally, and skillfully turn, skid, splash, and brake from behind the wheel of a brand new BMW. Every class is a revelation for drivers. Feel the thrill of the power and acceleration, and the wind whistling through your hair.

The next time someone has something caustic to say about your driving, you'll at last be faced with a viable alternative. Tell them to go to the BMW Driving Performance School, or you can tell them to go to hell.

The BMW Performance Center is located at 1155 Highway 101 South, Greer. Class reservations are taken by calling (888) 345-4BMW (4269) or visit www.bmwusa.com/performancecenter.

Where's the Grits?
Greer

There're only a few places left in South Carolina today where those stone-ground grits are made the way they were in days of yore. What a pity. Yes, of course, you can buy grits at every grocery store and some of the gift shops too, but grits that have been ground before your very eyes with the slow turning of a water-powered grist mill wheel are something else. Make no mistake. There's a real difference.

Suber's Corn Mill is one of those places where you can buy all you want and not only that, watch it all happen. They ought to know how to do it; the same family has been making grits here since 1908. Here's where they guide water from a holding pond through a trough to a large paddlewheel which turns slowly and powers a set of gears that move massive stones cut in the shape of wheels. The top millstone moves slowly, and the bottom stone does not move at all. But in the center of the top millstone is a hole through which shelled corn is slowly poured. What comes out of the bottom falls into a chute ready to be packaged and weighed by hand for eager consumers who know

The magic of old fashioned waterpower
can grind out grits and memories.

the difference between this and what that Quaker guy in the store has to sell.

Nobody knows why these special grits are more magically delicious or why they cook up so well, but something about eating homemade grits when it means the home they have come from is a grist mill makes a difference. It's always worth the trip you make to get them. *Homemade* grits means your Mama loves you. *Stone-ground* grits means you are a connoisseur.

Suber's Corn Mill is located at 2002 Suber Mill Road in Greer, just a few miles from Greenville. Visit www.scmills.com or call (864) 877-5616 for directions and store hours.

The Mysterious Pardo Stone

Inman

In 1935 most South Carolinians were preoccupied with surviving the Great Depression. It was a difficult time for everyone but harder still for the farmers who scratched out a living from the rocky soil of the Upstate. W. Bryson Hammet was one of those farmers harvesting grain on his farm near Inman (Spartanburg County), when his tractor bogged down and got stuck. In the process of digging out the foundered tractor he uncovered a stone, seventeen and a half inches long, twelve inches wide, and four to five inches thick. A week later he returned to the scene and noticed that same stone had mysterious markings. There appeared to be a date, 1567, and something that looked like an arrow, plus a parallelogram, and another symbol indicating the sun. Who made these markings? Could this date be real? Could it be a hoax? After all, the Depression was a time when people were desperate for money and distraction.

Nobody knew then, and nobody knows now. The most viable theory today is that this stone was left by a party of Spanish conquistadors who explored the Carolinas in the mid-sixteenth century. It's a fact that Spanish explorer Juan Pardo led an expedition through this area between 1567 and 1568 with intentions to establish a series of settlements between here and Mexico to transport gold and silver from the Americas back to Spain. But the actual meaning of the inscriptions themselves has eluded definitive analysis, and the only thing not in doubt seems to be the authenticity of the markings. The stone itself now rests in the Spartanburg Regional Museum of History, where someday it is hoped future archaeologists can yet decipher and further illuminate this cryptic message from the state's distant past. Visit www.spartanburghistory.org/museum or call (864) 596-3501.

Lake Be Dammed

Irmo

Lake Murray has long been considered one of South Carolina's best assets, and one of the state's most underutilized destination points. The lake is forty-one miles long and about five miles wide at its widest point, with breathtakingly beautiful (prejudice intended) and amazingly clear water.

The dam was a WPA project on which construction began in 1927 and was completed in 1930. The project provided hundreds of jobs for area workers during the Depression. It involved acquiring hundreds of tracts of land and relocating more than five thousand individuals' homes. The dam was finished and water began to collect shortly thereafter. The original intention, long ago lost in history, was to be a hydroelectric impoundment and to create electricity for neighboring Columbia and its surrounds. At the time it was completed, it was the world's largest earthen dam, and it created the world's largest man-made lake. The lake has 650 miles of shoreline, meanders through four counties, and totals forty-eight thousand acres.

For safety's sake, a backup dam was constructed and was finished in 2007. SC 6, which crosses the dam connecting Irmo and Lexington, was widened and a 1.7-mile walkway was then added. Not only is it a restful walk, you can see the Columbia skyline eleven miles away and the sparkling lake. Sunsets here are pretty spectacular too. Park on

Prepare to be awestruck: The pent-up strength of the Lake Murray Dam pushing back all that water is almost palpable.

either side of the dam at the SCE&G (South Carolina Electric and Gas) Recreation Areas (parking fee is $3) and take a stroll.

Now, just a word to the wise, as you are taking that stroll across and back. South Carolina can get really, really hot in the summer. Wear a hat. Drink plenty of water. Take your cell phone for one simple reason. You might need to call a taxi.

For more information about recreational options at Lake Murray, visit www.lakemurraycountry.com or call (866) SC JEWEL.

It's a Bird . . . It's a Plane . . . It's a Hurricane!
Lake Murray

Well, actually it's one bird, the purple martin—in flocks migrating in numbers of hundreds of thousands. From late June through early September, up to a million of these birds have chosen to roost, rest, and feed on a small twelve-acre island in the middle of Lake Murray near

The Weed from Hell

South Carolina does not have a state weed, but if it did, kudzu would win, hands down. As an attentive visitor plies the state's roads, it is difficult to miss multiple spots along our highways and byways where this green growth has completely taken over: not only trailers and barns, but telephone poles and trees. Yep. Sometimes it blankets everything.

We have a number of parasites that we celebrate and encourage, such as Spanish moss that gracefully blankets the trees of the Lowcountry, wafting in the breeze. Surely you have seen the obligatory shot that the television cameras make during golf tournaments such as The Heritage where Spanish moss frames the shot. It is an iconic part of who we are. But kudzu . . . puleeeze! If Spanish moss is cheese grits, then kudzu is raw brussels sprouts.

You cannot kill it. As soon as you cut it down, or try to dig it up, it magically reappears right next to the wheelbarrow that you were using to haul it away. When it takes hold of a piece of property, it acts just like your mother-in-law sitting down in your favorite chair . . . it will not budge.

Columbia, before embarking on the arduous journey to their winter havens in Mexico and South America. There are so many, in fact, that when they leave their island roost early in the morning for a day's foraging, the density of the birds in flight is discernible on Doppler weather radar, and the image has been likened in size to Hurricane Hugo, which devastated South Carolina in 1989. Similarly at day's

Some years back, Clemson University (South Carolina's agricultural school) tried to make kudzu into a bio-fuel, such as ethanol. As you might expect, Clemson was given a grant by Congress for this study. Oh, nobody howled about this gross misuse of tax dollars, because the source of the grant was Ol' Strom himself. Senator Thurmond, who was allegedly about 116 at the time, thought it might sit well with his old alma mater if it worked, and Clemson might name a cow barn for him.

When the results of the study came in, it was discovered that it took five units of kudzu to make four units of fuel, exactly the same ratio as corn to ethanol. But Congress in its infinite wisdom decreed that since Iowa led the nation in presidential primaries, corn would trump kudzu in the manufacture of fuel.

Nevertheless, South Carolinians still whack back their kudzu and wonder what might have been. Someone asked the Clemson professor who was in charge of the project what his cultivation scheme had been. "The process is both simple and mildly dangerous," he replied. "You dig a hole, throw some seeds in the hole, and run."

end the returning birds come in from all directions and form a circular flight pattern over the island like a black tornado descending into the safety of the small trees and shrubs roosting for the night.

The purple martin is a member of the swallow family and feeds on flying insects during daylight hours. In fact many people encourage the purple martin to take up residency in their backyards and waterside playgrounds to provide Nature's free insect control. Inventive man-made martin houses dot the landscape all over South Carolina.

The destination chosen by the birds is known as Bomb Island. During the early days of World War II, the island served as an artillery target for pilots practicing their bombing runs. Some call it "Doolittle Island," named for General James "Jimmy" Doolittle, the World War II ace, who led his Columbia-based Doolittle Raiders on the first air attack on Tokyo during the war. The presence of unexploded ordnance prevented the island from being inhabited after the 1940s and thus, it became a safe environment for wildlife. By the 1980s the island had been discovered by the purple martins, and the rest is ornithological history. In 1995 the island was designated as the nation's first purple martin sanctuary and is one of the largest roosting sites in North America.

To see the spectacle up close, join other nature lovers on the Carolina Wildlife Care Purple Martin cruises offered every week in July and August on a charter boat, the *Spirit of Lake Murray*. Call (803) 772-3994 or visit www.carolinawildlife.org for reservations and more information.

Fill 'er Up with Yesterday
Landrum

The advent of America's interstate highway system effectively homogenized the country's roadsides. The typical driving experience is one long, boring view of grey concrete and endless green medians punctuated by equally similar rest stops and refueling plazas.

★ ★

Stopping for gas in the old days was high adventure. Travelers often encountered "filling stations" as individualistic as the entrepreneurs who owned and operated them. Amazingly, in Landrum, South Carolina, there's an old time Esso Gas Station that turns back the clock like an episode of the *Twilight Zone.* It appears to be authentic from its signage to the discreet separate outhouse located in the back. It stands there, just off South Trade Street, in defiance of time and even reality. (To prove that, gas prices on the sign are posted at nineteen and twenty-three cents, but no one is there to sell gas at that price or any other.) This three-dimensional collection of architecture, signage, petroleum technology, and kitsch is there as a testament to the hobby of local enthusiast, Mack Henson, whose grandfather owned and operated the business for many years.

While visitors to this site feel like they've stepped back in time, this exhibit is actually a work in progress. People who find their way here get smitten with the project and contribute ideas and additional arti-facts to the collection, which is still growing. The single gasoline pump, for example, is one such addition. The refueling process required elbow grease and a strong bicep, but the pump worked well. Fuel was drawn up from an underground reservoir and filled a large, glass mea-suring tank perched atop the pump. Markings on the glass identified the amount desired, which was then fed into customers' vehicles by force of gravity.

Don't expect a lengthy interpretation if you happen by the site. The flood of memories it may invoke, and the questions it tends to inspire, are purely your responsibility and for your personal enjoyment. But the Old Esso Gas Station in Landrum is worth seeing. Leave I-26 at the Columbus, North Carolina, exit and head east on SC 108 (Lynn Road) until it branches. Stay to the left on 108 toward Tryon. Come to a stoplight, bear to the left, and you'll be on US 176 North (Trade Street). Through the small town of Landrum, the road turns into South Trade Street near the state line. The station will be on your left.

✦ ✦

Lest We Forget
Ninety Six

South Carolina has a plethora of heroes and patriots whose names we learn as children.

We follow their lives and feats of derring-do sometimes at the expense of the anonymous ones—the forgotten soldiers who did the legwork and faced the bullets head on. Raise a glass to James Birmingham who we know lived on Penny's Creek off Long Cane Creek in present day Abbeville County. The only other thing we know is that he fell during the 1st Battle of Ninety Six, which was fought November

The commemorative marker to James Birmingham pays homage to his patriotism and valor.

19–21, 1775. According to records kept at the time, he was the first Southerner to die for his country in the American Revolution. Rest in peace, James.

Ninety-Six Miles from Where?

Ninety Six

Visitors to South Carolina are often puzzled when they see the town named "Ninety Six" on their maps of Greenwood County in upstate South Carolina. This unusual name for a municipality always prompts the question—"How did it gets its name?" The romantic version is a favorite of many. It involves an Indian maiden who during the Cherokee War of the 1760s learned of an impending Indian attack on the

Colonial Ninety Six was a springboard for South Carolina history-makers in all directions.

British garrison. She supposedly rode ahead to the British camp to warn her English lover of the imminent danger. To mark her way she named the streams along her route and found her soldier at the trading post at the ninety-sixth stream.

Romantic as this story may be, it seems far more plausible that another legend might be closer to the truth. This one tells of a surveyor general named George Hunter, who first mapped this area of the state in 1730. As he made his map he marked the location "Ninety Six." It was assumed that meant it was 96 miles from the lower Cherokee Indian town of Keowee (near today's Clemson, South Carolina), and the name stuck. The trouble with that theory is, by contemporary measures, it simply isn't true. Ninety Six isn't ninety-six miles from anywhere in particular. Whatever the truth is, this quirky name for the quiet Southern town has endured and is likely to remain unchanged. Change, they say, is anathema here in the South.

Those Mysterious Hills
Northern Greenville County

Not every state has an area that seems to have evolved differently from the rest of the state. But South Carolina has a section where the enlightenment of progress, economic success, and educational promise somehow didn't shine in. It's called the "Dark Corner." The boundaries of the Dark Corner are nebulous and hard to define, but like the proverbial elephant in the room everyone knows it's there. Generally speaking when you're in the northwest corner of the state in the vicinity of northern Greenville County, you're there.

This is a part of South Carolina that became home to a subculture of rebellion, lawlessness, superstition, and fear—the result of poverty, isolation, and a kind of naiveté. The area was first settled by Scots-Irish immigrants whose land was granted to them by the King of England before the American Revolution. Many of those original land grants are now subdivided into a myriad of parcels owned by the descendants of the same families. The transition was not always friendly. Hard times begat economic stress, and one of the few ways these families could make a living was to make and sell liquor from their corn and rye. This was a skill the Scots and the Irish brought over from their homelands with pride.

As early as President George Washington's administration, an attempt was made to levy taxes on homemade spirits. He appointed "High Sheriffs" to collect these revenues for the government, and soon these men were called "revenuers." This pitted the moonshiners against government agents and what quickly evolved was an era of lawlessness. Many revenuers hiked into the misty mountains of the Dark Corner in an effort to clean up the mess but were never heard from again. Soon anyone who wasn't from *there* was considered an outsider and was suspect and unwelcome. Even ideas from outside the Dark Corner were untrustworthy, so political and religious thought followed suit. The legal and moral travails of the Dark Corner notwithstanding, nothing injured the pristine beauty of these mountains themselves and the verdant forests that clung to the hills. By the end of the twentieth century, a new light began to shine in the Dark Corner. It came with the advent of upscale mountain retreats and retirement communities centered on this lush scenery that offered easy access to southeastern metropolitan centers.

The Dark Corner will always be a colorful chapter in the larger story of South Carolina. Many say the Dark Corner is a concept of the past, and nothing at all remains from its era. But occasionally a whiff of smoke from a distant valley raises the question of whether one of the locals is putting up a few gallons of moonshine just for old time's sake.

★ ★

What's behind the Name?

Pickens

There's a 1,647-foot-high monolith close to the town of Pickens that rises out of the flat earth like a giant wisdom tooth breaking through the gum at a painful place. Since this area was settled by Europeans, it's been known as "Glassy Mountain." The truth is it's not made of glass. Instead, it is solid granite and anything but transparent. The little known story goes . . . a number of small springs near the top of the bare north face anoint the mountain throughout the year with a glistening cascade of water. This constantly falling water catches the Carolina sunlight and sparkles like cut glass—thus the name Glassy Mountain. So you'll know.

Not a pane of glass on the whole
mountainside yet the name endures.

Revolutionary War Re-enactors Take Heart

More Revolutionary battles and skirmishes were fought in South Carolina than any other colony. Keep your uniform clean and your powder dry. There may be another call to arms at almost any time.

Timing Is Everything

Rock Hill

It all seemed so possible; everything was falling into place. The engineering was solid, the design was bold, the entrepreneur was passionate, and even the financing was in line. It was going to be an automobile manufactured and marketed from South Carolina. Yes, it was an affront to Detroit, which was making most of the cars driven in America, but all signs were encouraging. After a few successful prototypes the previous year, the Anderson automobile assembly line began in earnest in 1916.

As a would-be automobile magnate, John Gary Anderson had good credentials. He worked through several careers before settling on the manufacture of horse-drawn buggies, and he learned the value of fine workmanship and quality engineering. In fact his Rock Hill Buggy Company set the industry standard for craftsmanship and grew to be one of the leading manufacturers in the South. By 1911 they had produced eighty thousand buggies and had raked in $6 million in sales. Nevertheless the automobile was overtaking horse-drawn vehicles, and by 1914 buggy sales had dropped by a third across the nation.

★ ★

**South Carolina's dream of replacing
Detroit, the Anderson automobile**
IMAGE FROM ORIGINAL COURTESY OF THE SOUTH CAROLINA
STATE MUSEUM, COLUMBIA, SC

To take on Detroit, Anderson had to lock horns with Henry Ford himself and build a car that would challenge the reliable and low-cost Model T. Anderson's insistence on quality and his limited scale of production seemed prudent as quality had served him well in the manufacture of carriages and buggies. By 1917 the company had realized $1 million in sales and had in hand orders for 1,200 cars. Anderson and his fledgling motor car company survived World War I by manufacturing small trucks and trailers for the war effort. Post-war sales in

1920 seemed healthy; Anderson built 1,280 automobiles that year, but big trouble loomed on the horizon. In 1922 Anderson's bottom price for a car was $1,195. In contrast Henry Ford sold a car with proven reliability for only $298. This disparity made all the difference and ultimately rang the death knell for the Anderson Motor Car Company. In 1926, after ten years and manufacturing 6,300 automobiles for the American market, the company shut down the production line.

This was after all just before the Great Depression, which changed the dynamic of American life in almost every way possible. The last thing we needed was another luxury automobile when millions of Americans didn't know if there would be any food on the table for their next meal. All that remains of the Anderson automobile today are a couple of early models in private collections, another at the Antique Automobile Museum in Myrtle Beach, and a sporty sedan at the South Carolina State Museum in Columbia. South Carolina was left with a broken dream of becoming a viable competitor to the thriving Motor City of Detroit and a sad, poignant story about what might have been.

A Tale of a Town

Rock Hill

Once upon a time there was a lovely little town called Ebenezerville. It was a quiet and peaceful place near the North Carolina/South Carolina border, not too far from Charlotte. One day in 1852 the mighty, mean, ole Railroad decided that they would build a rail line connecting Augusta, Columbia, and Charlotte to improve the shipment of the cotton crop from South Carolina fields to market. They proclaimed that Ebenezerville would be on the route. "Wait just a minute!" exclaimed the townspeople of Ebenezerville. "The big, noisy locomotive will frighten our people! And all that smoke, well, that is just not tolerable."

Lo and behold, the Railroad decided to avoid the uproar and bypass Ebenezerville, moving the track to a rocky location several miles away. The rocky knoll proved to be a challenge, but they persevered and

★ ★

named the place "Rock Hill." The new town grew and prospered and prospered and grew some more until, eventually, it encompassed Ebenezerville (now called Ebenezer), and they all lived happily ever after. The End.

South Carolina Seasonings for the Tongue

Salty language isn't associated with any state in particular, but South Carolinians use their peppery language in unusual ways. If your ear catches some of these phrases, here's a brief translation of some of the most common examples you're likely to hear.

1. That dog won't hunt. Go sell that notion to someone else.
2. Too wet to plow. Although the rain has stopped, it is too wet to cut the grass.
3. It's raining cats and dogs. See #2.
4. It's a frog strangler. Ditto.
5. T'reckly. It'll be another moment or two.
6. Uglier than a train wreck. Do not take her/him any place with fluorescent lights.
7. Dumber than a box of rocks. Ain't too smart.
8. His dog is on the porch. He's home.
9. Doesn't know the meaning of quit. Actually, he doesn't know the meaning of many words.
10. When you see bogey, take it. When you are in a hole, quit digging.

Up, Up, and Away
Simpsonville

For reasons that aren't exactly clear, South Carolina has not embraced the techno-hobby craze for hot air ballooning like some states have. It may have something to do with an excess amount of hot air from our own climate, political hot air notwithstanding, but no one really knows why ballooning never took off. But instead of a lot of smaller weekend flights by a scattering of balloon enthusiasts, South Carolina has one festival that rises above all the others and deflates all pretenders to the throne. It's called "Freedom Weekend Aloft," and it's held over Memorial Day Weekend every May in Simpsonville's Heritage Park.

The Simpsonville event is one of the largest hot air balloon gatherings on the planet. Competitors and enthusiasts come from all over the country, and as many as fifty colorful balloons can be seen taking to the air at any given time.

Competitive flights appeal to those skilled pilots who can negotiate the wind currents and accomplish feats or maneuvers according to the assigned task. Best of all, the airborne adventures are not limited to the attending professionals. Individuals can buy rides with tickets sold in the special balloon ride tent on the launch field. During sunrise and sunset hours, the optimal time for easy launch and descent, passengers can take rides lasting approximately one hour and travel up to fifteen miles away from the launch site. Riders may skim along the treetops and even float up to three thousand feet into the air. A chase car follows the wind-directed adventure on the ground and greets passengers upon landing with congratulations and a traditional glass of champagne. This is not an inexpensive endeavor; a one-hour journey into the sky can cost around $175.

On the other hand there are balloon adventures called tethered rides during which the balloon remains tied to a series of ropes that are connected to the ground. As the heated air gently lifts the balloon, riders enjoy the sensation of noiseless flight for several minutes. And then as the air cools, they effortlessly descend back to the ground. This

Something about the color and gigantic size of the
balloons plus the promise of an otherworldly view
of the earth below is simply irresistible.

can cost as little as $10 for adults and $5 for children, twelve years old and younger. The whole weekend is filled with contests, competitions, concerts, presentations, and themed celebrations, which all add something special to this patriotic holiday in honor of those in uniform past and present.

Freedom Weekend Aloft at the end of May may be a doorway to the dream of Phileas Fogg in *Around the World in 80 Days*. Or, at the very least, it's an entrée into the colorful, graceful, soaring world of hot air ballooning, a sport for the whole family.

Heritage Park is located at 861 SE Main Street in Simpsonville. Visit www.freedomweekendaloft.org for detailed directions and ticket information.

Pop Goes the Nickname
Spartanburg

Spartanburg, South Carolina, is no different from most of the other cities throughout the state in that it has a curious nickname. They call it "Sparkle City." Turns out the name comes from a 1950s rockabilly singing group known as Joe Bennett and the Sparkletones from nearby Cowpens. They recorded a jump tune in 1957 that made the hit parade and got them on *The Ed Sullivan Show* and the coolest of all places, *American Bandstand*. The TV shows and the singing group are, alas, all gone, but the nickname lingers on.

Order Up Food and Fun
Spartanburg

When customers first decide to visit Spartanburg's Beacon Drive-In, it's usually because of the stories they've heard and can't believe on first blush. First off this is a hamburger joint that's a throwback to the 1950s. No kidding. One almost expects to see bouncy cheerleaders in letter sweaters twirling pom-poms. The Beacon claims to serve three thousand hamburgers a day—that seems as credible as a snowball in hell. Add to that a blind guy taking care of the orders and keeping it

Super-size your nostalgia at The Beacon.

all straight by just calling them out to the kitchen crew. That's a lot to swallow.

The line to get in may be stretched out into the parking lot but fear not, it keeps moving. Once inside there are two first impressions. One is the anticipation that Elvis might appear at any time, and the second is the domination of a distinctive voice as the order taker relays the food choices to the hectic kitchen behind him. By the way, be ready with your order or risk a tongue-lashing here—time is precious at The Beacon. Even though he is blind, the order taker never seems to make a mistake as he calls out the orders to twenty or so food handlers working the production line. It may seem like chaos, but then the rhythm becomes apparent—this is a symphony, and there is a fascinating harmony taking place. Don't forget to order the famous Beacon Tea, a combination of sugar, tea, and lemon, so sweet you can cut it with a knife. Don't even think about ordering un-sweet tea. In South Carolina that constitutes a gastronomical sin.

Once seated, there's plenty of time to enjoy the ambience. Plastic furniture in orange and green, plus walls adorned with tributes to local athletic teams and civic clubs set the stage. Locals enjoy paying homage to these tributes, some dating back several generations.

The landmark lighthouse outside is just the prelude, so pull in, get in line, and partake of this flashback show of funk, '50s fun, and fabulous fast food. To find The Beacon, get off I-26 at exit 22 and, as directed, "just keep going for a couple of miles . . . you can't miss it." It's at 255 John B. White Boulevard. Visit www.beacondrivein.com.

Finding South Carolina's Oldest Bridge
Travelers Rest

After the American Revolution ended, South Carolina was feeling its oats for expansion and further development into the Midlands and Upstate. To do this they needed roads for commercial growth as the newly designated state's rivers tended to be short, shallow, and not easily navigable. One of the visionaries who saw this need was Joel R.

High road to history

Poinsett, a statesman who was then serving as director of the South
Carolina Board of Public Works. He envisioned a toll road extending
from Charleston all the way to the mountains terminating in Asheville,
North Carolina, a major feat of engineering at the time.

The road required the building of three key bridges in the northern part of the state. These were complicated projects all their own.
Of the three spans that were actually built, only one survives today.
This medieval-looking stone structure has a signature Gothic arch and
reaches across Little Gap Creek in northern Greenville County. Made
of native stone this distinctive castellated structure has endured largely
intact through the passing of time. It is thought to have been designed
by Robert Mills, who was America's first Architect General and a major
contributor to America's early architectural heritage. He is celebrated
today as the designer of the Washington Monument.

★ ★

After the bridge was finished in 1820, it was named for Poinsett, who later became ambassador to Mexico. He is mostly remembered for introducing America to a colorful tropical plant he found in Mexico, now called the "poinsettia" in his honor.

The bridge is no longer in use but is part of the 120-acre Poinsett Bridge Heritage Preserve located off US 25, thirty-nine miles north of downtown Greenville. To get there from US 25, turn right onto Old US 25 just past SC 11. Turn right on Callahan Mountain Road near North Saluda Reservoir. Poinsett Bridge will be on the left. Visit www.dnr.sc .gov for more information.

Pick a Town, Any Town

Let's face it; no one wants to live in Cut and Shoot, Texas. But South Carolina has some towns with crazy-sounding names too. We got your Possum Trot, which is lovely this time of year. And there's Cat Head, but people there are a little standoffish. There's Norway, Denmark, and Switzerland, if your passport's up-to-date.

If you're into math, you might move to Six Mile. There's also Nine Times (but you only have to go once.) There's a place called Round O, but everybody there seems a little dizzy. There's Thicketty, but they've got too many rabbits. There's even a place called North, South Carolina, for the directionally challenged.

Eureka might be exciting for some people. Fair Play's great, but you can't get away with anything there. There's actually a place called Sugar Tit, but we don't know much about it; our mothers wouldn't let us go there.

★ ★

A Cheesy End to a Lofty Dream
Walhalla

After the railroad's quirky introduction in Charleston in 1830, the attractive promise of cheap, fast transportation to the Midlands, the Upstate, and lucrative Northern market took off like a skyrocket. (See "The Hiss-tory of the *Best Friend*," page 189.) Numerous railroad companies took shape and reached out for their piece of the pie. One of these was the Cincinnati and Charleston Railroad Company, which built a line from Charleston to Anderson, Pendleton, and West

Mining a mountain for blue cheese?

Union with plans to go across the Blue Ridge Mountains. The physical and financial stumbling block was a peak named "Stumphouse," a 1,742-foot-high monolith of solid blue granite. The challenge was too high to go over, too far to go around, so the only solution was to tunnel through it, a task beyond the railroad company's financial reach.

In 1852 however, another company had the same dream. The Blue Ridge Railroad took up the challenge and hired 1,500 workers, the majority of which were Irish immigrants. They built a town called "Tunnel Hill" nearby to house these workers and their families that eventually had stores, a church, school, post office, saloons, and even a burial ground. With only sledgehammers, crude drills, and dangerous black powder, they managed to dig 1,600 feet into the mountain when operational funds ran out. Then came the War Between the States, and the dream of a tunnel through Stumphouse Mountain seemed over.

In the 1940s however, a professor from Clemson College discovered that conditions inside the unfinished, abandoned tunnel were just right for curing blue cheese. The environment inside the tunnel was always 56 degrees with 85 percent humidity, and that criteria became the basis for a university product, Clemson blue cheese, now famous throughout the state and beyond. The dream of piercing Stumphouse Mountain resulted in a crumbly, strident, and slightly tangy happy ending. Today the City of Walhalla maintains a park at the site, located about seven miles northwest of Walhalla on SC 28. Visit www.oconeecountry.com/stumphouse for more information.

Lions and Tigers for Rent Oh, My!
Wellford

If you need a pair of cooperative lynx for a Mercury automobile commercial, where do you get them? Or a friendly zebra for a pantyhose ad? How about an understanding rhinoceros for a Land Rover ad campaign? They have to come from somewhere. That's why there's Hollywild in Wellford, South Carolina.

★ ★

The wide world of wild animals is closer than you think.
KIM ATCHLEY, HOLLYWILD ANIMAL PARK

It all started with the Meeks's family farm in Spartanburg County with a collection of farm animals that included horses, cows, chickens, and goats. The collection grew from there to include native South Carolina critters like squirrels, foxes, opossums, and raccoons. Young David Meeks grew up amid this backyard menagerie and found a natural affinity for working with animals. One species at a time this collection expanded to include an adopted Asian elephant, tigers, bears, lions, deer, swans, monkeys, and more. David and his father soon opened what was called M & M Zoo and welcomed visitors who loved interacting with the animals. By 1985 David bought out his father and created an animal park eventually called Hollywild dedicated to education of the public. Even Hollywood noticed David's skill at handling this diverse population. He was a wrangler of the first order. In time he supplied the film industry with animal talent for sixty-five movies such as *Prince of Tides* and *The New Adventures of Pippi Longstocking.* His animals were also featured in TV spots, brochures, conferences, and private parties. He's even supplied the camels, donkeys, and lambs for Christmas nativities on occasion.

Hollywild is located at 2325 Hampton Road, Wellford. Visit www.hollywild.com or call (864) 472-2038 for more information on their Outback Safari Ride through more than seventy acres, home to more than five hundred fascinating animals. Feeding stations throughout the park allow visitors to participate in a care and feeding program that is both fun and educational. This includes the bottle-feeding of baby calves whose eyelashes will warm your heart.

index

index

index

index

index

index

Lee Davis Perry

Native South Carolinian Lee Davis Perry was raised in Charleston and returned to her beloved city in 1987 after pursuing her education and a nine-year stint away in "the urban fast lane." Lee received a journalism degree from the University of Georgia in 1976 and did graduate work there in public relations. In 1979 she began her career in Atlanta, working for several ad agencies, among them J. Walter Thompson USA, where she was a senior media planner.

The pull of the ocean and the traditions of her childhood proved too strong to abandon for long, though: "Who says you can't go home again?" Since returning, Lee has worked as a freelance advertising and marketing consultant on local and regional accounts, creating and implementing many award-winning campaigns. In 1997 she joined J. Michael McLaughlin as coauthor of *Insiders' Guide to Charleston* and was instrumental in bringing about ten more editions of this best-selling city guide. She has collaborated with Mike on articles for national magazines as well as numerous business presentations. In 2009 she penned *More Than Petticoats: Remarkable South Carolina Women*, a collection of brief biographies of outstanding women from her home state, another volume in Globe Pequot's popular series.

Lee and her husband, Rhett, divide their time between the Lowcountry and the Midlands of South Carolina, renovating an old house (ca. 1803) in Charleston's historic district or relaxing on the serene waters of Lake Murray. Both locales provide the perfect settings to contemplate the timeless beauty, vitality, and diversity of the Palmetto State.

about the authors

J. Michael McLaughlin

J. Michael McLaughlin has been living in and writing about the Low-country for more than thirty years. During that time his interests in history, architecture, and the legendary Charleston lifestyle have led him into countless adventures.

His writing has found its way into numerous regional and national magazines, such as *Modern Maturity* and *Diversion.* His freelance work as an advertising and public-relations consultant has captured national marketing awards. In 1992 he was one of the originators of the four hundred–page *Insiders' Guide to Charleston,* an in-depth and comprehensive introduction written for visitors to his favorite Southern city. Incredibly, time and appreciative readers have resulted in twelve additional updates, now sold nationwide through Globe Pequot Press. He was joined in 1997 by Lee Davis Perry, with whom he coauthored the last ten editions.

Michael was raised on a farm in Indiana, but he's quick to point out it was in southern Indiana, and "in Charleston, that makes a big difference." He graduated from Indiana University in 1967 with a B.S. in business-journalism, aiming for a Madison Avenue career in advertising. Instead, his first writing job turned out to be in Vietnam, where, as a war correspondent, he won a Bronze Star (exceptional meritorious achievement) for his coverage of the 101st Airborne Division during the ill-fated 1968 Tet

After a decade back ng writer-producer for several Midw e writer col-ony in Key West, Florida. An vh 19 's Hurricane David forced h di d Charleston. Ever since, h a and the Lowcou char

Other books ho Barada) inc. 4, and a novel.